YOUR FIRST

1000

· C O P I E S ·

The **STEP-BY-STEP** *guide to marketing your book*

TIM GRAHL

Book Design & Illustrations by Lauren Baker

Printed in the United States of America

First Printing, 2013

ISBN 978-0615796796

Out:think Group
PO Box 4112
Lynchburg VA, 24502

www.outthinkgroup.com

YOUR FIRST 1000 COPIES

TO THE THOUSANDS OF AUTHORS WHO HAVE MADE MY LIFE
BETTER THROUGH YOUR WORK. I HOPE THIS HELPS YOU
REACH MORE PEOPLE.

TABLE OF CONTENTS

INTRODUCTION

Imagine if you had a direct connection with thousands of readers who loved reading your books. And imagine if those readers eagerly awaited the launch of your next book. How would that direct relationship with your readers change your writing career? How would you feel knowing that every time you started a new book project, you already had people excited to buy it and ready to recommend it to others?

Many of today's most loved and successful authors know what those experiences are like. I know they do because I've worked with many of them to build their online platforms that connect directly with readers. For over four years, I have worked with bestselling authors such as Daniel Pink, Charles Duhigg, Dan Ariely, Pamela Slim, Chip and Dan Heath, Ramit Sethi and more. I've also worked with first time and self-published authors such as Gene Kim, Michele Ceres, Noel Yeatts, Garret Kramer and others to get their platforms started from scratch. In all, I have worked with over a hundred authors as well as studied and interviewed many more.

Thanks to this experience, I know exactly how reader relationship building works and how to use those skills to sell more books. You can learn these same skills.

Now, more than ever, you have access to all the tools you need to connect with readers without investing in expensive tactics like hiring a publicist or going on a thirty city book tour. Why then aren't more writers successful at selling books? Because the problem isn't the availability of resources; the problem is knowing how to use them to get results. With too much advice swirling around about blogging, Twitter, podcasts, forums, Facebook and others, most authors are left spinning and confused about what to do when and where to start.

This short book will solve that problem by providing a clear, actionable and proven system to author platform building, the same one that today's bestselling authors use as the key ingredient in their book marketing.

A platform is whatever plan and method you use to connect with your readers and sell books, whether it's traveling the world to speak, hand-selling to friends or building a popular blog. From my work and study, the authors selling the most books today are those that are focusing first on planning and building their platforms.

With this book, I'm going to empower you with a step-by-step plan on how you can use online marketing tools to build your platform.

The heart of this plan is the goal of connecting you with your readers, spreading your ideas, sharing your journey and using your writing to add value to people's lives. We are going to look at tools like blogging, email marketing, social media and others. Regardless of the individual tool, however, the goal is always to establish a connection with your readers that will last a lifetime and support your long-term writing career.

Your writing makes people's lives better. The more people you connect to your writing, the better this world will be. As we proceed through this book, I will show you how to build these long-lasting connections that will sell books in a way that is natural, comfortable and fun for both you and your readers.

I have named my step-by-step plan the **Connection System**. The fundamentals are so strong and simple that every author can immediately implement this system after reading this book to begin building their online platform.

Our journey into online platform building will start with the best way to get **Permission** to communicate regularly with your fans. Then we will discuss how to engage your readers through **Content** that you will make freely and widely available. Once you have permission and content, we will examine how to find and connect with new readers through **Outreach**. Finally, we will talk about how you use Permission, Content and Outreach to naturally and ethically **Sell** your books. In each of these sections, we will talk about how to **Track** everything you are doing so you can see what works and what doesn't.

The Connection System is how authors are working for and

earning their success in today's evolving publishing marketplace. Whether you are just getting started in your writing career or are a long time author struggling to figure out how to step into the new era, this book will lay out the plan you need to get your platform up and running so you can reliably and predictably build an engaged readership and sell your first 1,000 copies.

Let's get started.

**WHAT IS
MARKETING?**

- WHAT IS SELF PROMOTION? -

"What about that one?"

The salesman's smile faded just a bit as I pointed across the parking lot.

My wife and I were at the car dealership with our three-month-old son preparing to make the decision that would officially crown us as parents.

We were buying a minivan.

When we first arrived and began walking around the lot, the salesman couldn't tell us enough good things about the brand new models that had just hit their lot. They looked great and had all the features we were looking for with the exception of the hefty monthly payment.

That's when I glanced across the parking lot and saw a few of the last year's models and asked our salesman about them. He reluctantly led us over and allowed us to take a look. He didn't have a lot to say all of a sudden as we inspected the vehicles. From what we could tell, last year's models were almost identical to this year's models, except they were $10,000 cheaper.

The purchase decision was a no-brainer: We chose a last year model, which fit much better into our budget while not compromising on comfort or quality. To this day, our minivan has been a wonderful vehicle.

But what was the salesman's problem?

And why is it that this is the picture that so often comes to mind when authors start thinking about marketing?

Why don't we like the sleazy car salesman?

What exactly is it that turns us off?

We could discuss his sales tactics—the lies and half-truths he told. We could talk about his pushiness and attempted hard close. But all of that boils down to one simple fact: He wasn't looking out for our best interest.

Trust is a fundamental part of any friendship. My best friends are those that tell me the truth whether I want to hear it or not. Friends are people that are willing to tell me when I'm making stupid decisions as well as encourage me onward when I'm making smart ones. A friend has your best interest at heart, always.

What if a friend was helping you buy a new car? How would

the experience be different than with the sleazy salesmen?

Would a friend try to talk you into buying a car you can't afford? Would a friend stretch the truth to trick you into a brand new model you don't need? A friend might get pushy, but only when she thinks you're about to make a mistake.

The fundamental difference between someone you trust and someone you don't is your belief in whether or not they are looking out for your best interest above their own. The bottom line is plain: When someone isn't looking out for your best interest, that means they're only self-promoting their own.

- MARKETING REDEFINED -

Let's be clear about what we're trying to achieve with the Connection System before we get into too much detail.

If you look up the definition of "marketing" in the dictionary, here's what you'll find:

"The total of activities involved in the transfer of goods from the producer or seller to the consumer or buyer, including advertising, shipping, storing and selling." [i]

That's too broad and outdated a definition to be useful for what today's audience-oriented authors like you are trying to do.

Let's try out this revised definition:

"The act of building long-lasting connections with people."

That's it. That's the complete definition for how today's authors successfully market their books and is the underlying principle of this entire book.

The more long-lasting connections you make with readers, the more books you will sell in a natural manner that reflects genuine connection rather than shady salesmanship.

- RELENTLESSLY HELPFUL -

We've all had those moments where you finish a book, close the cover, set it down and think, "My life will never be the same." *Purple Cow* by Seth Godin ignited one of those moments for me.

At the time, I was a 23-year-old and had just started my second job out of college. I should have known that this new job was destined to be a mistake when I showed up for my first day and they were cleaning out a closet for my office. I was hired to be a software developer for a local direct mail and fulfillment company. However, on day one, I was told that they needed me to work in the printing room for "just a couple of weeks."

Three months later I was still there with no end in sight.

Frustrated, I started Googling around for new career ideas. I soon found Seth Godin. His ideas about work and careers were so inspiring that I picked up his book *Purple Cow* on the way home and read it straight through to the end. Thanks to Seth, I immediately realized that there were better options for my professional life than my closet office and running a giant printer.

A couple weeks later I worked up the nerve to email Seth and ask him a question. I fired it off assuming it would vanish into the in-box abyss never to be seen again. But low and behold, within the hour, Seth emailed me back with a thoughtful answer.

Amazing.

I soon learned that this warm and responsive behavior was normal for him.

Every day he publishes at least one blog post. Every day he answers reader emails. Every day he thinks of new ways to positively influence the world. His writing and his ideas have changed the lives of thousands, if not millions, of readers like me for the better. Consequently, when Seth's next book or product launches, I willingly purchase it because I am so thankful for how relentlessly helpful he has been and continues to be. He has created an excitement within me to continue learning from him.

Through his reliable blog, email and other writing, Seth has created a long-term connection with me that results in me buying at least one copy of every book he releases.

- SO WHAT IS MARKETING, REALLY? -

Let's sum up what marketing is and should be.

Marketing isn't sleazy car salesman tactics.

Marketing isn't tricking people into buying.

Marketing isn't unethical.

Marketing isn't intrusive self-promotion.

Marketing is two things: (1) creating lasting connections

with people through (2) a focus on being relentlessly helpful. Does that seem so bad?

- SYSTEMS, SYSTEMS, SYSTEMS -

When I began working with a business coach a few years ago he immediately stressed the need to create systems and checklists for my company.

This didn't make any sense to me at first. Why would a company of two people, myself included, have a need for systematizing the way we work? We weren't a huge company (we still aren't) and we never wanted to be encumbered by bureaucracy that slows things down.

However, trusting my new coach, I put aside my skepticism and began implementing some of his ideas. To my great surprise and delight, the results were amazing.

I learned that by systemizing my workflow with a checklist or automated set of events, I freed up more quality time to focus on other areas of the business. While my trustworthy system took care of the mundane and repetitive tasks, I was able to concentrate on new ideas and opportunities to grow my business.

Like my business coach taught me, I'm going to teach you how to systemize your book marketing workflow for improved results.

If you create the right processes and checklists, they will free you up to write more quality content and connect more frequently with your readers, all while your trustworthy system does your marketing for you.

- YOUR TOOLBOX -

If I wanted to build a new house and you were kind enough to supply me with a toolbox of the latest and greatest equipment, would I be fully set up for success? Not likely considering I have a hard time using a hammer without smashing my thumb. Even if I gave the project every best effort I had, I would not be able to build a credible house.

Owning the tools is not enough.

To be successful building anything, you first need to have a blueprint for what you're building. Second, you need to select the best tools to get the job done. And third, you need to learn how to properly wield those tools for maximum effect.

It's not about the tools.

It's about what you are trying to build and how you build it.

- YOUR INTERNET MARKETING TOOLBOX -

The Internet offers you a great wealth of marketing tools to consider using as you build your online author platform.

Social networking platforms such as Twitter, Facebook, Google+, and LinkedIn.

Blogs.

Email marketing.

Guest blogging.

Interviews.

Speaking events.

Blog commenting.

Online forums.

Podcasting.

Any technology, media type, channel, or interaction opportunity you use to engage with people for your online platform is a valuable resource that goes into your toolbox. Choose the tools you use carefully as they are not one-size-fits-all solutions. The trick is to identify your platform's unique characteristics and needs so that you learn how and when to use the right tools.

- IT'S NOT BAD ADVICE -

Here's the typical timeline.

An author hears how she should be using Twitter to market her book so she Googles "How to market on Twitter" and starts reading the articles that pop up. After a few minutes of reading random advice, she has a vague understanding of how to promote her work on Twitter, creates an account and starts posting to Twitter. After a few days, weeks or months, frustration sets in as the results she expected seem non-existent. Her follower count is low. Nobody is sharing her posts. Her book isn't selling.

She feels like she's sending tweets in a vacuum.

This frustration finally hits a tipping point and she gives up. "Twitter just doesn't work for me," she tells herself. Is this true? Was the advice she discovered and followed about marketing on Twitter bad?

Maybe. Maybe not.

If I read a couple articles on how to use a hammer correctly, would I be any closer to building a house? Not really. I need a plan for what I'm building before learning when and how to use the tools.

Knowing how to use a hammer is not enough.

Knowing how to use Twitter is not enough.

- WHAT'S THE PLAN? -

Josh Kaufman released his first book *The Personal MBA* in December 2010. He did exactly one speaking event for the book. He had no major media coverage. He never hit any of the major bestseller lists. And yet, in just over two years after releasing his book, he has sold over 130,000 copies of his book.

How is this possible?

He has a great system.

Every author has a plan to sell his or her book. Most of these plans, however, are rarely good because they rely on surrendering direct access to readers to others. These typical plans go something like this: Release the book. Pay a publicist. Run as fast as you can to get as much media coverage as possible. Hope the PR blitz converts to sales. Once the initial media push dies out, however, book sales die off. That's when these authors start working on their next book. Here's a rough graph of this approach to book marketing:

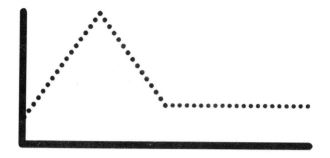

Josh's plan was very different. Months before the book came out, he built a system that would steadily and predictably move people to buy the book over a long period of time. Here's a rough graph of Josh's book sales:

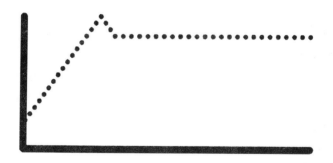

Josh's system works with very little input from him. Imagine if you had a book marketing system that worked the same way. What would your writing career look like if each book you wrote and published had a system around it that kept it selling year after year?

Before you launch your next book, you need a plan on how you're going to engage with people before your book is available, and then motivate them to buy your book once it's published.

By the end of this book, you will have that plan.

- THE HOLEY BUCKET -

Most authors have a holey bucket problem.

They go out and work really hard (or pay a publicist to work really hard) to get people to know about their book. However, when the work (or money) pays off and people visit their online platform, there is nothing in place to create a long-term connection with those readers. Could they buy a copy of the author's current book? Sure, but what about the next book? How will these same readers know when the next book is ready to debut? More importantly, how will they be invited to purchase that next book?

Without a way to start a long-term relationship with your readers, your customer lifetime value shrinks dramatically. Consequently, you will end up working harder (or paying more money) for fewer results. Ultimately, the long-term readers you could have had simply leak through the holes in your bucket, possibly never to return again.

Or as one of my clients said, "Tim, it's not that I have holes in my bucket. There's no bottom to the bucket at all!"

- PLUGGING THE HOLES
WITH THE CONNECTION SYSTEM -

Plugging holes in a physical bucket is straight forward, but plugging holes in your online author platform is often a much greater mystery.

The best way to plug your platform's holes is to create a system that, as people hear about you for the first time, funnels your readers' attention into a system that allows you to reliably stay in contact with them over time. As you nurture those long-term connections by being relentlessly helpful, book sales will naturally flow.

Once you have this plan defined, the time has come to pull out your marketing toolbox and select the tools to build your Connection System. Your personal Connection System is your answer to your holey bucket problem; it will lead your readers down an engagement path that has no dead end and many opportunities to buy your book. First things first, we need to plug the holes in your bucket with the primary ingredient of effective online platforms: Permission.

- WHAT IS MARKETING? -

Marketing isn't sleazy or slimy. It's the opposite. Good marketing focuses on creating long-lasting connections with people and looking for ways to make their lives better.

CHAPTER TAKEAWAYS

. . . .

Good marketing is first and foremost about helping people. Make this your focus and book sales will naturally follow.

. . . .

Creating a marketing system will free you up to be more creative.

. . . .

Never focus on the tool. Instead, develop a marketing blueprint and select the right tools to build it.

. . . .

The Connection System gives you the confidence in marketing so you can create the long-term connections with readers.

- PERMISSION -

Without permission, your communication efforts risk being ignored, deleted or otherwise tuned out. To put the odds in your favor, seek permission from your readers before you start connecting with them. When you have earned such permission from your readers, be sure to respect that permission by communicating with them in a way that is reliable, authentic, value driven and encouraging of action. After all, permission-based communications are the opposite of spam.

Ultimately, permission is what you use to plug the holes in your bucket because permission fosters conversations that will last long into the future. These conversations with your readers are what interest them in the subjects you are writing about, which leads them to buy your books. No advertising costs or frustrations required. And if you have a system in place that establishes permission with readers, the book sales will follow naturally.

In today's marketing world, what is the best tool for getting permission to communicate with your readers in a way that reliably gets their attention and encourages them to take action?

An email list.

- FROM NOBODY TO BESTSELLING AUTHOR -

Ramit Sethi shouldn't have been a successful author.

In 2009, he was a 24-year-old kid who had no publicist or media attention of any kind: radio, television or newspaper. And yet, when he launched his book *I Will Teach You To Be Rich*, it immediately became a *Wall Street Journal* and *New York Times* bestseller.

What did he use to make that happen?

His email list.

Now, three years later, Ramit runs a thriving online business that makes over a million dollars a year teaching people how to earn more money, find their dream jobs and negotiate big raises. What does he use to market his products?

His email list.

Ramit isn't the only author today using email to drive book sales and succeed in their career. In fact, many of today's bestselling authors develop large email lists. Why are email lists so important and powerful? Because an email list is the perfect way for a reader to give permission, thereby creating the direct and reliable communication channel between reader and author that is the foundation of the Connection System. This is how authors stay connected with their readers in a way that gets attention and drives action.

Readers don't just casually give their permission, however. Permission must be earned by offering a valuable and credible incentive. Earning such permission is the art of motivating website visitors to grant permission to stay connected. A unique breed of person knows how to do this very effectively: Internet marketers.

- WHAT DO INTERNET MARKETERS KNOW? -

If you start researching the world of Internet marketing, you'll quickly come across names like Frank Kern, Brendan Burchard and Jeff Johnson. While I don't recommend or endorse all of their tactics and products, they are interesting case studies in ways to effectively sell products and make money, especially using online platforms.

The email list is their most preferred tool because it generates the best results by a wide margin over any other tool. In fact, if you were to ask them to choose between their email list or all of their other marketing assets combined (Facebook, Google+, Twitter, their blog, their podcast), they'd pick the email list every time. The reason is simple: Their email list is where they make their money.

- IT'S SURPRISING -

I was reluctant to believe in the power of the email list when I first began working closely with authors. At the time, I thought email was on its way out. The advent of blogging eliminated your need for a web programmer to help you get your words published to the world. And the rise of social media gave you direct access to the same platforms millions of people were logging into every day. How could email possibly keep up?

However, the more I worked with, talked to and studied successful authors, the more I saw email playing a central role in their platform strategies. *"Is there a common reason for this trend?"* I wondered. As it turned out, there was: Having a direct connection to an individual's inbox gives authors a way to communicate to their readers where they regularly spend their time.

- DIRECT ACCESS -

Reaching people where they're already spending their time is important because the world has become a busy and noisy place. Every day, people are confronted with sales messages they aren't interested in and stories they don't care about. What they do care about are the few direct relationships they've invited into their lives. Such direct access is the essence of our new marketing definition: "The act of building long-lasting connections with people." It's very important that you think about the strength and integrity of that connection. Always give readers meaningful reasons to continue giving you their attention and following through on your calls to action.

- MOVING PRODUCTS -

Escape From Cubicle Nation author Pam Slim leads one of the most passionate and engaged tribes of readers I've ever had the pleasure to work with and experience. Her email list, Twitter and Facebook platforms each have strong numbers. So when I recently helped her launch a new video course product, I was curious to see which asset would perform best in converting to product sales. We marketed her course to her email list and to her social media connections, all the while watching the numbers. The result was staggering: For every one sale Pam received through social media, she received 50 sales through her email list.

- WHY DOESN'T SOCIAL
MEDIA WORK AS A SALES TOOL? -

Email seems old school compared to social media and other more recent inventions of the changing Internet marketing world. But while social media is more popular, email is more effective. To understand why, you must realize that most people interact with social media and email in vastly different ways.

For example, when was the last time you read every tweet in your Twitter stream or every update in your Facebook newsfeed or every pinned item on Pinterest?

Now consider, when was the last time you skipped reading an email that made its way into your inbox? Two wildly different answers, right?

The difference between your two answers explains why social media is an ineffective sales tool: Most people only choose to see and consume a tiny portion of the content that fills their social media channels because those channels are fire hoses of information. In contrast, email is still a manageable connection channel that we all regard as more private.

I run an ongoing, unscientific survey with friends and colleagues that validates these behaviors. On average, they admit to reading only about 1% of the total social media updates that fill their feeds. I then ask them how many of their emails they read. The response is usually close to 100%.

Industry math shows why we have adopted these behaviors. Twitter users generated 200 million updates a day in June 2011.[ii]

At the same time, three million photos and the same number of messages were being posted to Facebook every 20 minutes.[iii]   Today, those numbers are much higher.

Given the flood of information flowing through social media, email remains the most direct and reliable way to get in front of people in the digital world.

- YOU CAN TAKE IT WITH YOU -

Facebook, Twitter and the other social media platforms are notorious for making changes to their platform that make marketing harder. They also don't let you easily move to a new platform because they block you from downloading your fan's contact information. For example, you can't log into your Facebook Page and download all your fan information so that you can contact them outside of Facebook. Although platforms like Facebook are useful in many ways, remember that if you build your tribe on other platforms, you are beholden to those platforms for all time.

However, if you build an email list, you *can* take it with you. You built it therefore you own it, which means you have direct access to your reader's inboxes from anywhere. If all else fails, you can turn on your computer, open your email client and send everybody a message yourself. That may not be the best solution, but if it comes to that you have at least succeeded in not giving up control of your most important marketing asset: the connections with your readers.

- YOUR #1 GOAL-

As an author, your survival depends on your platform: your ability to create long-lasting connections with readers and get them to take action. Long-lasting connections depend on the quality and reliability of your email list. If you nurture your email list with engaging content and protect their privacy from spam, then your readers will reward you with their time and attention. Because those rewards are essential to driving book sales, your #1 goal as an author should be to grow your email list as much as possible. Write that on a post-it. Recite it to yourself every morning. Tattoo it on your forehead. Do whatever it takes to make sure that developing your email list is the #1 goal of your platform strategy.

Let's now explore precisely how to achieve that goal.

- GETTING YOUR EMAIL LIST STARTED -

Before you can begin growing a list and sending emails, you must first select and set up your email marketing tool. Smart authors use web-hosted platforms like MailChimp, Aweber or Constant Contact instead of personal email clients like Outlook or Gmail. Why? Because software like Outlook and Gmail doesn't easily facilitate list building; you would have to do it all manually. Also, your emails will start getting blocked, spam reports will spike and readers will get frustrated if there is no easy way to unsubscribe. All told, using software like Outlook and Gmail for email marketing is inefficient, ineffective and likely to violate Federal CAN-SPAM laws.[iv]

To me, the choice of which tool to use for my email marketing is like choosing someone to repair my broken toilet. For my toilet, I could choose the quintessential handyman, though that option always scares me. When something goes wrong at home, I don't want someone that is kind-of good at a lot of things. I want someone that is the best at the one thing I need fixed. If my toilet is broken, I want the best plumber. And when I want to build an email list, I want the company that is the best at email marketing.

MailChimp, Aweber and Constant Contact are just the beginning of many options. The industry is competitive with each provider vying for your attention and choice. Here's what you need to look for before you sign up with anyone.

- **Useful features.** Does the provider offer useful features such as detailed reports on email open rates and click rates, professional email templates and customization options?

- **Ease of use.** Is the platform easy to use? Granted, any technology can be frustrating at times. Choose the one that is the least frustrating.

- **Free or cheap.** Is there a free or nearly free option for someone who is just starting out? Many providers allow you to build your initial couple thousand subscribers for free. Make sure you compare prices before making a decision.

- **Ongoing innovation.** Has the company recently released new enhancements of its technology? Stagnation can be a real problem with some email marketing platforms. They reach a point where they think their product is "good enough" and then stop innovating. Make sure you choose a company that demonstrates innovation.

- **Help and Support.** Does the provider offer online tutorials and videos that teach you how to use their platform? Also, do they have live chat and phone support staffed by competent, eager people with a great attitude? You can always call their support team before you're a customer, just to evaluate the quality of their customer service.

I have a lot of experience with email marketing platforms. Because the technologies change so frequently, and because new providers enter the market almost as often, I did not want to recommend a specific tool here in the book because that would be hard to update in the future. Instead, please visit www.first1000copies.com/email to get my latest recommendation on the best tool to use for email marketing.

- MAKE AN OFFER THEY CAN'T REFUSE -

There are two overarching rules for getting lots of people to sign up for your email list: (1) make a specific, compelling offer and (2) expose them to the offer multiple times.

Many writers struggle with the first rule because they use generic language like: "Sign up for my news and updates." This kind of language doesn't explain what you're inviting people to receive. That confusion is bad because it doesn't create a strong impulse to subscribe. Specifically, such vague language fails because it doesn't give a good reason for someone to subscribe or explain what they get when they do. With an offer of "Get my news and updates," are you really compelling someone to grant you direct access to their inbox? Probably not.

Instead, focus on what's in it for them. You need to make a very specific offer that addresses a very specific need or want. For example, if your readers need an alternative solution for improving their work habits, then offer a weekly newsletter series that offers one specific action they can apply immediately each week that will build into a positive, lifelong habit. This offer needs to be clear so that your readers understand what they will get out of joining your email list. Such understanding is key to providing a "win-win" situation where they get something of value while you get something of value.

Once you have a strong offer, you need to share it multiple times. Many writers stunt the growth of their email list because they only make the email list offer in one place, like the sidebar of a website or blog. One time is not enough. Decisions that affect one's privacy, like giving someone their email address, require convincing. One of the best ways to convince readers is to expose them to the invitation many times. The authors that do this well have a signup form featured on their platform's homepage, a dedicated content page for their email list offering, a sidebar feature, and/or a signup opportunity at the end of every blog post. In each of these cases, the value proposition of the offer is made clear so that the reader is most likely to consider subscribing.

- WHAT CAN THEY EXPECT, AND WHEN SHOULD THEY EXPECT IT? -

When Jean Chatzky, author of *Money Rules* and financial editor for NBC's Today Show, hired us to increase her newsletter subscription rate, the first thing we looked at was the signup offer. The original copy was similar to "Get news and updates." That wasn't going to cut it, especially since Jean wanted to start sending out a weekly email sharing a useful review of what was happening in the financial world. We worked hard on the offer, eventually deciding to go with "Jean tells you what the week's headlines mean for YOUR wallet." The result was incredible; by the end of the first 12 months following the update, her email signups had increased 332% over the previous 12-month period.

DIYWOD.com provides another striking example about the power of clear, value-driven offers. DIYWOD.com sends customized workouts to subscribers on a daily basis that they can do at home. The headline at the top of their website says "Get daily workouts customized for you." With that sharp of a headline, nobody is surprised when they start receiving daily emails containing a great workout that can be performed at home. The offer is clear and the delivery meets expectations.

You need to be equally clear and value-driven with your email list offers. Let your readers know what solution you're offering and when they can expect to receive it in their inbox. Are you going to email daily, weekly or monthly? Are you going to solve a problem or provide something desirable? Whatever you have to give, make it as easy as possible for your readers to receive, and make sure it is clear when they should expect it to arrive.

- GIVE SOMETHING AWAY -

Danielle LaPorte tells the "white hot truth" on her website and is the author of *The Fire Starter Sessions*. When you visit her website there is an email newsletter subscription box at the top of the site that reads "SUBSCRIBE and you'll get The Strategy of Desire Worksheet from my book, *The Fire Starter Sessions*." While this offer is less clear about what you'll get on an ongoing basis, it's extremely clear about what you'll get right now when you sign up. This approach is very effective for those authors that are unsure about what they may be able to deliver in the future but have a valuable, one-time offer to give today. Offers of this type are particularly successful because instant gratifications are always compelling and interesting.

- DON'T HIDE YOUR EMAIL SIGNUP FORM -

Even if you have an amazing offer, you won't get many people subscribing to your email list by putting the signup form in the footer of your website. Or if you use the exact same color, size and font for your signup form as everything else on your site. Or if you bury the form in the sidebar with five other things.

The email lists that attract the most signups are those that are the most attractive. You need to make yours stand out by using vivid colors, fonts and other design elements that draw the eyes toward your offer. If your signup form can't do that, then don't expect a lot of signups. Bottom-line: make your signup form hard to miss because it's the gateway for readers to give you permission to stay connected with them.

Therefore, put your signup form at the top of your site. Put it on every page. Design it to stand out. Use contrasting colors. Use images. Put it after people comment on a blog post. Put it at the bottom of every blog post. Put it at the top of every blog post. Do whatever it takes to make sure readers are seeing and considering your offer.

- DRUNK SURFERS -

In a February 2012 blog post titled *The $5 Guerrilla User Test*, Xianhang Zhang describes how he likes to go to bars to test out new website usability designs. His method: buy someone a beer and then let them click around the website. Why does Zhang want slightly drunk people playing with his websites? Because the web browsing behaviors of slightly drunk people are similar to how we surf the Internet at any given time. According to Zhang:

> Users aren't so much unintelligent as they are distracted and indifferent. Your average user may be perfectly competent and zip through your [website] like a charm when they're in a controlled setting, focusing exclusively on your [website] and incentivized to succeed. But such a scenario is almost never likely to happen in the real world. What's more realistic is that they're devoting, at best, 10% of their attention towards your [website] while they have the TV blaring in the background, an IM conversation they're also involved in, thoughts about whether that meeting with the boss tomorrow means a promotion or getting fired. Your [website] is at best, 5th on their priority list and they're largely moving on autopilot as they navigate through it. Once you understand this basic reality, user behavior becomes a lot easier to understand.

This "distracted and indifferent" behavior proves why you can't bury your email signup form in your website footer or hide it in the sidebar. Make it hard to miss. And make it easy to use. For example, keep the amount of required fields low. If you only really need their email address, then only ask for that. Asking for their first name, last name, address, or some other piece of personal information is an additional distraction and reason not to subscribe.

- HOW DOES THE INTERNET WORK? -

You can't get to the homepage of Forbes.com without seeing an advertisement. When you're halfway through reading a *New York Times* website article, a box flies across the screen inviting you to buy a subscription. YouTube features an advertisement across the top of their site as well as plays a minute long advertisement before I can watch the next cat video. A giant ad slides down a few seconds after I visit HuffingtonPost.com. These are some of the most trafficked sites on the Internet. What does this mean about the nature of advertisements on the web?

It means that, for the majority of people using the Internet, *this is how it works.*

We grew up understanding that commercial breaks were a natural part of the television experience. Users of the Internet today assume the same thing: that content owners are going to make the most important things for them hard to miss. Therefore, what matters is not *if* you should promote your email list or book on your author platform, but *how* you should do it for the best results.

- HOW TO INCREASE SUBSCRIPTIONS -

It took me a full year to talk him into it, but finally Daniel Pink, best selling author of *To Sell is Human* and *Drive*, agreed to let me put a popup on his site to encourage more subscriptions to his email newsletter.

A popup is a visual box that displays on top of the content on a website, typically featuring a strong offer and casting the website's content into the background. Popups get the most visceral arguments and reactions from my clients and colleagues because one common stereotype of such tools is that they're too aggressive. Such people tell me that popups are "too pushy" and "annoying," while others tell me that "they interrupt my reading!" Individuals like this often believe that "people hate popups" and that "I'm going to get tons of hate mail if I ever use one."

These emotional reactions are very real and I do understand them. The problem is that such feelings are not backed up by verifiable data. In contrast, I have data that proves that popups work extremely well as a tool to promote email subscription signups. At this point in my career working with bestselling authors, I've installed dozens of popups across many sites. On average, the response is incredibly positive: massive improvements to the email subscription rate with basically no negative impact to site traffic or reader satisfaction.

For example, I started working with Daniel Pink in December of 2009. At the time, he didn't have an email newsletter so that was, of course, the first thing we set up. The list grew at a steady rate for the first 25 months. I was then able to convince him to install a popup. During the four months that followed, we added 50% more subscribers to the newsletter. That's the same amount of growth in four months as we had gained in the prior year.

How much hate mail did Daniel get for installing the popup?

None. How much did his website traffic go down? None. Did Daniel see any negative results whatsoever? No. And as a result, he became a believer in popups as a smart way to grow his #1 marketing asset.

- HOW TO DO POPUPS RIGHT -

I've developed a few rules of thumb over the years of testing and interacting with popups. These will help you stay on a positive course as Daniel did, reducing the risk of any sort of negative backlash. Remember, popups are effective tools that can be used for good. Here's how:

- **Follow all the previous rules.** Be specific with your offer. Make it compelling, and consider giving something away for free.

- **Put it on a delay.** Don't have your popup trigger the instant a visitor lands on your website. Wait at least 20 seconds before you show the popup. This delay allows your visitors to engage with your content before you put an offer in front of them. Most people leave a site in less than five seconds, so if they have stuck around for half a minute, you have them engaged.

- **Only show it once.** Once the visitor has seen the popup, don't show it to them again for a very long time whether they subscribe or not. If you constantly interrupt people every time they load a new page of your website, the experience will be annoying. However, if you only offer the popup once, then they'll either accept or not and move on.

Since you're not a web programmer, you might be scratching your head wondering how you're going to install a popup, set it to display on a delay and limit it to one occurrence. Because popup technology is similar to email marketing technology—both industries see a lot of change—I created a page on my website for my favorite popup recommendation. If you're interested to try a popup on your site, please visit www.first1000copies.com/popup to learn more.

- WHY GREAT CONTENT MATTERS -

After using these email list-building guidelines, you'll likely see a big increase in signups. Now that your audience is growing, you may be asking yourself, *What do I do next?* The answer lies in the story of the bad car salesman I shared earlier: look out for your customer's best interest.

Readers join an author's email list because they want to learn something interesting and useful. You serve their best interest by satisfying that curiosity with great content sent on a regular basis, content that matches whatever you claimed in your offer. Fulfill the promises you made when they signed up to your list, and focus on being relentlessly helpful every time you send an email.

Delivering value in this way does two things for you.

First, it makes the connection with your readers stronger than ever. They'll look forward to your next email and know that every time you show up in their inbox you have something good to share.

Second, if you know that you are regularly sending out great content to your list, then you'll gain more confidence to invite other people to sign up because you know your readers are enjoying what you're sharing. Recruiting readers into your email list is not a sales tactic so you can trick them into buying your book; it's an invitation to build a long-term connection with you so that you can send them really great content.

If you focus on delighting your subscribers, it's easy to invite people to be a part of it.

- PLEASE HELP ME FIND A JOB -

Joshua Waldman runs CareerEnlightenment.com and is the author of *Job Searching with Social Media for Dummies*. He helps people use social media tools and Internet marketing techniques to find jobs. He's constantly looking for ways to be relentlessly helpful to his subscribers. New blog posts and new email newsletters go out like clockwork and are always packed with great content for people looking for jobs. He's even built an iPhone app, developed free eBooks and created online courses to help his audience. As a result, his book continues to be one of the top selling "For Dummies" titles. He's being hired to speak and consult more and more. And, generally, he's become the go-to person in his industry. Joshua has achieved all this because he is committed to being relentlessly helpful to his readers with quality content.

- STAYING IN TOUCH -

I worked with an author last year as he launched a book that hit all the major bestseller lists. You may not believe it, but this was his first book. I had built his site using Connection System strategies and tools in order to grow his permission asset off of all the publicity he was getting. Before long, we went from two people on the list (the author and myself) to thousands of people on the list. That's a fantastic result. But fast forward nine months and he hadn't sent a single email to his list since launching the book. That's not good. Sadly, that's very normal.

Many authors work hard to build their permission asset and then never send anything out to it. Such a lack of attention does all kinds of damage. For starters, the subscribers will forget about you and why they subscribed. When you finally do email them, probably when it's time to launch your next book, the subscribers will ignore it, unsubscribe, mark it as spam or all of the above. Even if they do read your email, they will have little reason to take whatever action you're suggesting, especially one that involves buying something. If you haven't invested yourself into your subscribers between book launches, they have no connection to you anymore and won't be compelled to buy your next book.

Remember, the goal of building your email list is to create a meaningful connection with readers—one based on mutual interest and quality content—that you work hard to strengthen with each new email.

- WHAT CAN WE LEARN? -

Annie Murphy Paul sends out "The Brilliant Report" to her email subscribers every week. She writes about how the latest research in neuroscience and psychology can make us better learners. Each report contains a short piece written exclusively for her newsletter subscribers as well as links to her favorite articles from the previous week, ones she's written and ones others have written. Annie's newsletters are always filled with very interesting thoughts and new discoveries. They're also a great update on what Annie is learning as she writes her next book.

Annie has made her email newsletter a helpful and interesting must-read for anyone interested in the science of learning. Thanks to her devotion to being relentlessly helpful, she's established a supportive relationship with her readers that works both ways. Annie supports her readers now with the information they're looking for and can't find anywhere else. Her readers will reciprocate that support later when it comes time for Annie to launch her next book or project.

- TELL ME A STORY -

CJ West is a self-published thriller author who does a lot of creative things to build and engage his email list. He offers Kindle giveaways, tells interesting stories, and shares the books he enjoys, among other things. Most recently, he built an interactive online thriller experience that allows you to choose your path through the world of one of his latest stories.

How cool and compelling is that, right? That's the sort of thoughtful creation that keeps readers happy and craving more. When you allow readers to immerse themselves in your content, they become part of the story too. Any author can do this, including you.

Once you have the connections made via your email list, start telling a story that readers can relate to and join. They'll love you for it.

- THE MAGIC FORMULA -

There isn't one. That may be sad news to some, but I assure you it's not. The true magic of using the Connection System to build your own platform is that you're in control of what happens. Based on the needs of your readers, the type of work you do and the nature of the industry you're in, you're empowered to determine how often you should email your list and what content you should put into each newsletter. That's a lot of responsibility, no doubt about it. But there is no opportunity without responsibility.

Thankfully, help does exist in the form of best practices. Experiment with these as you're putting the pieces of your author platform together. The best authors in the business use these with great effect. You can too.

- **Send enough to stay top-of-mind.** Don't let people forget you exist.

- **Focus on being relentlessly helpful.** Give great advice. Share the best content. Delight with new stories. Share reviews of the most recent books you've read.

- **Keep it personal.** Kill the corporate speak. Write your emails as if you were writing them to a good friend or colleague. This should be an email from you, not your PR department.

If you're still struggling with where to start, I recommend publishing an email newsletter twice per month. Send the emails on the first and third Tuesday of every month at 3:00 p.m. local time. On the first Tuesday, send something delightful such as a short piece written by you, a new video you created, or a sneak peek at your next book. On the third Tuesday, send an "author update" to let people know about your latest projects and where they can see other things you've recently written online. People signed up for your newsletter because they enjoy your work, so don't hesitate to let them know what you're working on now.

Keep that schedule for six months (12 issues), then reassess. You have to do it long enough to see if that structure is working and how you feel about it. Six months will give you a solid sample size of feelings and results to know if you're on a good path, or if you should adjust your path. At all times, remember to remain focused on staying in touch and being relentlessly helpful. Those principles will never change no matter what email publishing schedule you keep.

- A WORD ON STATISTICS -

The Connection System we're building through this book is intended to perform predictably and produce results that can be tracked. This data is important to capture and look at to make sure that the decisions you're making are ones based on evidence, not guesses. Your email newsletter is one of the best places to turn to for such quality data on your marketing efforts. Through your email list, you can see how engaged people are with your content and overall message.

For example, you can see which subjects are more interesting to them than others. You can figure out which days and times produce the best results. And you can discover trends that can tell you what to do more of as well as what to do less of. However, as with most sources of statistics, email list data is filled with more information than is necessary to pay attention to. To avoid burning out over the data, focus on these key statistics.

- **Open rates.** How many people are opening your emails? What is the percentage? If you're building your list in the right way, then your open rate should be at least 25% per email. That may seem low. It's not when you consider that single digit open rates are normal for most industries and companies. If you just started your list and it's still small, then the open rates are going to be high. Over time, as your list gets bigger, that percentage will drop. It should never drop below a healthy number, however, so long as you're promoting the list ethically and sending out great content. That said, be aware of false negatives—people that open your email but don't get counted—can occur. The technology that tracks open rates is far from perfect.

- **Click rates.** If your email newsletters don't contain any outbound links, then this statistic doesn't matter. You'd be smart, however, to link to at least one resource online where your readers may continue engaging with you or learn more on a given subject. If you are including links, it's useful to know how much attention those links are getting. This statistic can vary wildly from email to email depending on the objective of a particular email. As a general rule, shoot to have half of the people that open the email click on a link.

- **Subscriber rate.** How many people are signing up for your list on a daily and monthly basis? This statistic depends on the things you're doing to get your name out in the world. We'll explore that topic in great depth shortly. For now, keep an eye on how many people are joining your list and make sure that number grows in the right direction: up.

- PERMISSION IS EVERYTHING -

Establishing Permission to stay in contact with your readers is the cornerstone of the Connection System. When you look into your online marketing toolbox for the best tool for the job, your email list stands apart as the most effective. Gaining permission isn't a given; you're going to have to work hard to earn a reader's trust. Keeping that trust is even harder. So remain faithful to your list, constantly delivering value and offer new ways your readers can engage with you. If you approach the process with the right attitude and work ethic, your author platform is bound to grow and prosper.

CHAPTER TAKEAWAYS

. . . .

Make building your email list your #1 marketing goal.

. . . .

Sign up for an email marketing tool that is affordable and best in class.

. . . .

Be specific and compelling with your signup invitation offer.

. . . .

Make the email signup form stand out on your website.

. . . .

Use a popup.

. . . .

Focus on providing helpful, valuable and delightful content on a regular basis.

. . . .

Keep a schedule as to when you're going to send updates
to your list.

. . . .

Use your email marketing tool to track how many people
are signing up to your list, opening your emails and taking
action.

CONTENT

- WHAT TO DO WHEN YOUR BUCKET IS READY -

Permission is the cornerstone of your Connection System. Without permission, your system of building long-lasting relationships with readers won't work no matter what else you do. The best-selling authors I work with have embraced this idea to great success. But the success they enjoy doesn't come simply by having permission. The success comes from using that permission to deliver valuable content that readers anticipate receiving and look forward to reading. So, with the tools and techniques of permission marketing established, let's turn our attention to the next major element of your Connection System: content.

Content fills your bucket with readers eager to know you directly and benefit from your writing. You get the most people into your bucket by making your content as widely and freely available as possible. Sharing your adventure in this way will give people a path to interact with you and your ideas, which strengthens the bonds of your connection as well as encourages your readers to share your ideas with other people in their circles. Ultimately, you are giving them interesting ideas they can talk about, respond to and advocate to others. That's precisely how bestselling authors become bestselling authors: They spark interest in and demand for their ideas by giving away some of their most valuable content. Such freely accessed and shared information allows your name to escape your reader's inbox and enter the word-of-mouth world, which attracts even more readers to discover you and subscribe to your newsletter.

- SHARE FREELY AND PUBLICLY -

Publicly and freely sharing your content accomplishes many things as you work to grow the size of your platform. First, it allows people to interact with your writing before committing to giving up their email address or purchasing your book. This is an important first step in building trust with a reader. Second, it gives bloggers, journalists and other online content publishers something to link to. This promotes the virus-like spread of your ideas to readers you otherwise would have struggled to reach yourself. Third, it gives something for search engines like Google, Bing and Yahoo to index, which bring new readers through online search results. When you combine these three accomplishments—early trust from new readers, credibility from being linked to by other online authorities, and improved search result relevance—you become seen as a valuable and trustworthy author that cares about readers and is worth subscribing to.

Now that we know what we are trying to accomplish, what is the best way to do this?

- SHARING TOO MUCH -

Is it possible to share too much great content? I know many authors that have wrestled with this question. You may be wrestling with it too. It's definitely a common question, one driven by the fear that somehow you will give away so much content that nobody will be motivated to buy your books. As a partner to many authors and now an author myself, I completely understand this fear and why you have it.

Although this fear is legitimate, it is small and pales in comparison to the more important concern: releasing a book that nobody knows exists. As Cory Doctorow, bestselling author and founder of Boing Boing, said, "Obscurity is hard to monetize." Obscurity is the enemy that you should be worried about above all others. Therefore, hiding everything you create until it's bound together in a book is not a smart idea; you will be quite lonely when you start looking for readers once the book is published.

The solution is to share, and share widely. And deeply. And too much. Share until you become afraid that you're sharing too much, and then share some more. Sharing your content freely and publicly gives something concrete for readers to engage with and share, which introduces them to your work and allows them to become excited by it so that you can invite them to go deeper.

In all my experience working with authors, I have never seen or heard of an author that lost a huge amount of sales because they shared too much. Even when Adam Mansbach's illustrated book *Go the Fuck to Sleep* got released online in its full format, it only drove sales higher. More recently, Timothy Ferriss partnered with BitTorrent, a massive online file sharing network, to package his latest book *The 4-Hour Chef* with bonus content into a massive media bundle for free download. The result: two million downloads that drove 250,000 additional sales.[vi] The bottom-line: Sharing is how you build your platform. You can't build an effective platform without it. If you hide all of your writing until it has a price tag on it, you'll never create trust-based, value-driven connections with readers that naturally lead to book sales. Instead, you'll be stuck scurrying around trying to sell your book using all the overly aggressive tactics we've all come to hate. But if you start with sharing, you allow connections with readers to build and develop over a long period of time. This approach, the Connection System approach, protects you from needing to use the desperation tactics many authors suffer from.

The benefits from sharing your content wide and far can be tremendous. Having worked with and studied hundreds of authors, here are a few of the common themes I've observed:

- The authors that give away the most valuable content build the fastest followings.

- Giving away your best work is a direct path to building a lot of connections with readers.

- Making your content widely and freely available is the most consistent, sure-fire way of building attention for and engagement with your platform.

Sharing a lot of content freely and widely may always make you feel a bit uncomfortable. You're right to have that feeling, just don't let it consume you. Remember that the best rewards in work and life are reserved for those that embrace their discomforts and push forward. If you're afraid of sharing too much, keep it in perspective with the risks of obscurity. Obscurity is far, far worse. Do everything you can to climb out of that dark hole.

- TO BLOG OR NOT TO BLOG -

Attracting the attention of as many people as possible is the goal of creating and sharing valuable content. As readers engage with that content, they become more willing to consider an invitation from you to take the next step and give you permission to stay in touch directly. There are a variety of theories and tools to help you achieve this goal. Blogging is among them.

Without fail, "Should I have a blog?" is the first question I receive when I speak with authors about how best to publish and share their content. The nature of blogging offers many wonderful benefits: readers can leave comments on articles, you can share your personal story, and other websites and blogs can link back to your content, to name a few. But before you jump into blogging, keep in mind that a blog is just another tool in our toolbox. While I do like blogs, they aren't for everyone. What's most important is our goal: to make our content available widely and freely. With that in mind, we can look at the best tool to accomplish this: other people's platforms.

- OTHER PEOPLE'S PLATFORMS -

When I began working with Jeff Selingo, author of *College (Un)bound*, he was already writing as an editor for *The Chronicle of Higher Education* and as a blogger at LinkedIn, the popular online professional network. These platforms allowed him to put his content in front of thousands of people on a weekly basis, which perfectly matches up to our goal of sharing content freely and publicly to get in front of as many people as possible. If you have opportunities to create and publish content on popular platforms that already exist, the results can be far better than trying to start your own blog from scratch. So, as you consider the easiest and most efficient and effective way of sharing your content with the world, consider these questions:

Could you get stories published regularly on a popular website?

Could you get a weekly column with an online platform such as Forbes, Psychology Today, or The Huffington Post?

Could you get your short stories published in popular anthologies or magazines?

Could you work with an existing blog to provide weekly how-to articles for their readers?

There are a lot of websites, blogs, magazines and newspapers out there that constantly need new content for their readers. These platforms are great opportunities to share your content freely and publicly much faster and easier than you could likely accomplish by building up a brand new blog. As we'll explore next, however, this approach doesn't mean you don't need to build up your own sizable audience that you can communicate with directly. There is a way to do that without involving a personal blog.

- GREAT RESOURCES -

Chip and Dan Heath, bestselling authors of several books including *Decisive: How to Make Better Choices in Life and Work*, are self-described digital cavemen. They blog only a couple times a year and are not active on social media. However, they have been able to build a very big email list, which contributes greatly to their success as authors. How is this possible? In a word: resources.

For each of their three books, they created bonus resources that help readers take the subject matter of the book to a deeper level. These resources—like podcast episodes, PDF workbooks, audiobooks, and more—are all freely available on their website. But the only way you can access them is to sign up for their mailing list.

Although this strategy doesn't involve a blog, it still fits within the framework of the Connection System because it is rooted in high quality content that motivates readers to give their permission to be contacted about even more excellent content in the future. Chip and Dan simply choose to use book-specific resources as the form of content instead of focusing on creating a volume of content with a blog. For them, this strategy has been tremendously successful because that content is extremely helpful to their readers. That's the main point: Regardless of form, your content needs to be extremely valuable and shared widely and freely in order to build a large audience. And yes, if you don't want to create resources, you can blog.

- TO BLOG -

All authors need to carefully think about their unique situations when deciding which platform-building tools are best for them. For Jeff Selingo and the Heath brothers, they decided not to build personal blogs. But many authors do. In fact, blogging is still the most common technique for sharing content online. Thousands of authors use it successfully to spread their content and connect with readers. Therefore, authors should consider blogging when starting to build their platforms.

Starting and growing a blog has a lot of moving parts. We'll explore all of the essential elements together in the coming sections. Like email marketing, the first big decision revolves around which blogging tool to use. Here are a few important guidelines to apply to your evaluation of any blogging tool:

- **The tool should be free to get started.** Every good blogging platform lets you start creating and publishing content for free.

- **The tool should be easy to set up and use.** If you cannot go from signing up to blogging in very little time, then it's not the right tool for you.

- **The tool should support a wide selection of themes and plugins.** This allows you to easily add a new look and new functionality to your site along the way.

- **The tool should allow you to take your content with you.** You should be able to export all of your content easily and move it to a new platform if you ever need to.

I've worked with and evaluated a wide variety of blogging tools, including self-hosted WordPress sites, WordPress.com managed sites, Blogger, SquareSpace, and more. Each has strengths and weaknesses. Because the tools can change quickly given the pace of technology these days, I don't want to offer a single recommendation here that can't be easily updated later. So, similar to my email marketing tool recommendation, my latest blogging platform recommendation can be found by visiting www.first1000copies.com/blogging.

- AN ADVENTURE WORTH SHARING -

My favorite quote about blogging comes from the great Hugh MacLeod, bestselling author of *Ignore Everybody* and *Evil Plans*. His advice: "Treat it like an adventure, an adventure worth sharing." That's precisely the attitude successful authors have when approaching the process of sharing content, including Hugh on his popular blog Gapingvoid.com. If the content is not engaging, if it does not contain a story to follow, and if the story isn't leading up to a big event or moment (or series of moments), then the adventure is not worth being a part of.

Here's the secret: If you're an author, you're already on an adventure. You're reading and researching new studies and books. You're traveling to interesting places and meeting interesting people. You're making new discoveries that change the way you see the world. Even if you never leave your house or town, you're creating entire new worlds in your head and expressing them with your hands. All you have to do is tap into that journey and share the experience. Readers want to join in on your adventure. Give them one (or many) and they'll love you forever.

- WHAT HAVE YOU LEARNED TODAY? -

Derek Sivers, creator of CD Baby and bestselling author of *Anything You Want*, is a self-proclaimed learning addict. Reading loads of books is one of the main ways he learns. When he reads a new book, he takes lots of notes. When he first began this practice, he would organize his notes in text documents that he kept on his computer for easy reference. Later, he decided to post his book notes on his website Sivers.org. Over time, he has published more than a hundred highly in-depth book reviews that share the insights he learned while reading. His book notes archive is a treasure trove of fantastic content that attracts lots of new visitors to his website and has been a big reason his email list has grown to well over 100,000 subscribers.

The magic of Derek's content strategy is its simplicity. He was already creating valuable content for himself. And since he's not the only person on the planet to enjoy learning by reading books, that content is valuable to others. By taking a very small extra step—publishing that content on his blog—Derek invited readers into his personal adventure. He allowed them to see what he was reading and discover what he was learning. That shared experience is at the heart of Derek's personal Connection System with his readers.

- BLOGGING YOUR BOOK -

37signals is a software company based in Chicago, Illinois. They're small in size and large in influence and revenues. Since 1999, they have grown their *Signal vs Noise* blog (SVN) into a cornerstone asset and advantage for their business. 37signals uses that platform very effectively to recruit new employees, share their persuasive ideas and give sneak peaks of their products, all thanks to SVN's huge following.

In March 2010, 37signals founder Jason Fried and partner David Heinemeier Hansson published their first book *Rework*, which quickly became a bestseller. *Rework* is made up of an edited group of their favorite blog posts containing their best advice on how to run a business. There are many layers of adventure at work here. First, they used SVN to share their journey with readers. Next, they leveraged that asset to create a new one, the book, which serves as an adventure for people discovering 37signals' ideas for the first time. And what do you think happens after these new readers finish enjoying the book?

They start reading SVN for more. These many aspects of adventure convey an important point: Done well, an adventure offered through content builds a never-ending experience that keeps people in your bucket.

- DVD EXTRAS -

Derek Sivers and 37signals have shown us two ways that smart authors can tap into content that they're already creating during the learning and writing process. This begs the question: What are you already creating that you can use as content to grow your audience? One way I like to think of this is the special features or extras on DVDs. Using DVD extras as an example, I've come away with two interesting observations.

First, DVD extras include content that was either already created or easy to create during the filming process. Deleted scenes and alternate endings are usually added to DVD extras for precisely this reason. Additionally, DVD extras commonly include content like actor interviews and director commentary because this content is freely available during the filming process, it just has to be captured.

Second, DVD extras are made available for fans. If you hate a movie, you are unlikely to dive into the DVD extras. The extras are there for the fans because the fans want more and smart creators give fans what they want. Fans are the people that ultimately determine the success of a movie. And when you keep your fans happy, your next movie is set up for success too.

What I've noticed is that this exact same process can be applied to books.

Is your book full of technology and computer jargon that you had to research? Did you do a ride along with the police to get their procedure down? Were you exposed to a new way of doing business that you'd never seen before? What did you learn from those experiences that never made it in the book but that could be shared as extra content?

Similarly, did you interview professionals for your book? Could you make those interviews available in full? Or, could you do a follow-up Q&A with the interviewees?

Also, what got cut from your book that you could make available to fans? Were there chapters that got removed? Did the original ending change? How about that epilogue you thought about adding but didn't? Or special comments from beta readers that helped you shape the book into its final form?

Generally, what are the byproducts of your writing process? How can you make these available to your fans to let them engage with you and your work at a deeper, more meaningful level? That's the essence of adventure-based content that transforms the casual reader into a lifelong fan that will support your future books.

- RE-IMAGINING CONTENT -

Ann Handley and C.C. Chapman do an excellent job of pinpointing one of the major themes of adventure-driven content in their book *Content Rules*. They explain this theme as a simple idea: re-imagining content. In one form or another, the authors we just met have applied this theme to their content strategies because creating fresh content is hard to produce. Whether it's written words, speaking events, videos or anything else, brand new content is an extremely time-consuming and resource draining endeavor. And let's face it; your career requires more of you than just producing free content. The *Rework* authors need to run their software business. Derek Sivers needs to focus on the many projects he's involved with. Because their time is limited and precious, they've learned to be creative when it comes to producing and sharing content far and wide. You need to become as imaginative as them by re-imaging your content in new ways.

There are many ways to begin thinking about re-imagining your content. Can that talk you gave at a conference be transcribed and released on your blog? Can you take the interview with the subject matter expert and release it as a podcast episode? Can you share your book research notes or outlines with your email list, inviting them "behind the curtain" of your writing process? The possibilities are truly endless.

I'm working with an author right now on such a content strategy. For this project, we are leveraging the great work that's already been done in new ways to help grow his platform. For example, he wrote a whitepaper that consisted of 11 main ideas. We are using this whitepaper to convert people to the email list on his website. Next, we are taking the whitepaper and releasing it on other websites to introduce him and his ideas to new people.

Our re-imagining hasn't stopped there. We're also creating 13 different videos five to ten minutes each based on the content of the whitepaper (plus an introduction and conclusion), which we'll release as a series on popular video websites like YouTube. After that, we'll do a 13 part series releasing each of the videos as blog posts for his readers and to increase search engine traffic to his website.

The bottom-line of our strategy is exactly as Ann Handley and C.C. Chapman advise: By re-imagining one piece of content, we're able to create many more pieces of valuable content with very little effort. How can you do that? How can you re-imagine the content you're already producing to create and seize new opportunities to grow your platform?

- FANS WANT MORE -

I know that some authors worry about re-imagining their content. They're fearful that doing so will upset their readers out of the belief that readers only want completely new content all the time. Fortunately, that's not true. Your most engaged readers—your fans—want to engage with your content in multiple ways for multiple reasons. Some desire to have the message of your content reinforced. Others want to consume your content in different styles based on differences in their routines. And never forget that no two people are precisely the same when it comes to how they learn best; some learn better by reading whereas others learn better by listening or watching. To serve all of these needs, you actually must re-imagine your content in multiple ways.

And let's not forget the universal impulse of fans to over consume what they love. Being a big fan of reading myself, I love discovering a new author I like and then diving deep into all of his or her content. For example, I'll search iTunes for every podcast episode that he or she has ever been interviewed on. I'll read all of his or her books. I'll read all of his or her blog posts. I'll subscribe to his or her Twitter feed and email list. I'm a true fan to those authors I enjoy and care about most. Your true fans will show you the same devotion, but only if you give them the adventure-driven content to do so.

What I find wonderful from these experiences is that I appreciate hearing the author's ideas expressed in new ways. The blog posts will convey them slightly differently than how they are addressed in the podcast episodes. When I read the books, the content is fuller and a better narrative than the blog posts or emails. We all know that the whole is greater than the sum of its parts. That positive, uplifting effect is what's happening when you re-imagine and share your content in different ways.

- THE TRANSCRIBER -

All authors aren't quick to see and embrace this idea of re-imagining your content into an adventure that your readers can share with you. I met one such author several years ago who was very hesitant to adapt existing content. At the time, we were trying to build his email list and wanted to send out a new message every month. Unfortunately, I wasn't successful in persuading him to follow through on delivering valuable content on this monthly frequency because we simply didn't have enough content to share. As a result, his audience-building efforts suffered.

This author's hesitation was due in part to his belief that re-imagining content was a difficult process. As we've seen, that's not true. If you find yourself stuck with the same nagging belief, try this solution I created. It's simple, effective and easy to maintain, so long as you have a transcriber. This transcriber can be a friend, assistant or significant other that's on board to help out. Whoever the transcriber is, here's the process you two need to follow:

1. Set up a 15-minute phone call with your transcriber. Once you schedule a working meeting with someone else, putting off the necessary work becomes much harder.

2. Record the call. This transcript will be invaluable to the transcriber afterward when he or she is taking the first pass at creating content for you. If you don't have a good call recording solution, you can visit www.first1000copies.com/record to see the one that I use.

3. Tell your transcriber everything you want included in the content. Your directions don't have to be word-for-word. Just describe the content you want in outline fashion with some style elements mentioned too.

4. Instruct your transcriber to leverage this conversation into a draft piece of content that you can eventually publish. Your transcriber doesn't have to be a professional writer to make this solution work. He or she simply has to be able to add material to your outline.

5. Get back on the phone when the first draft is ready. Discuss the draft in detail and share any specific edits you want made. This conversation should probably be recorded too.

6. Publish the content on your blog or to your email list once the edits have been made.

If this process won't work for you, feel free to adapt it in a way that will. The most important thing is to find a workflow that removes any stress or hesitation you have about quickly re-imaging content for your platform. Remember, the Connect System model only works if you maintain those connections with content. That's the goal. If you need a helping hand to meet that goal, be sure to get one.

– Q+As –

The questions you receive every day are another amazing source of information that you can re-imagine into other forms of content. Do you get a lot of questions when you share your book ideas to family and friends? Have you already done a book tour or a few speaking gigs where you faced some interesting questions from readers? And what about social media; have followers sent you some thoughtful questions via Twitter or Facebook? The answers you give to those questions hold more value than in just answering the initial question; they offer value to your entire platform, but only if you capture and share them.

By turning these answers into content for your blog or email newsletter you accomplish several things at once. First, you write content you know your readers are interested in because they've already asked about it. Second, you save time and energy now because this content is quickly produced since you've given these answers before and probably have them already written down. In the case of questions by email, all you need to do is look back at your responses to get the content. And third, you save time and energy in the future because when new readers ask the same questions you can simply point them to the answers already available on your site instead of re-writing them every time.

Part of your adventure—the adventure you invite your readers to join through your content—involves the exchange of questions and answers. This exchange is a personal interaction that your readers enjoy because it lets them engage with you on a more equal and familiar level. For you, this exchange helps you identify themes that your readers are interested in, which you can turn into a future book or new content series. Ultimately, questions and answers are an important piece to the strength and development of your platform.

- 20% EXTRA -

"How am I going to find the time to do all of this? I'll never get my book written!"

This response is normal from most authors I start working with for the first time. I agree that the idea of regularly creating email newsletters, blog posts, social media updates, guest articles and other forms of content can appear daunting. But like many things in life, the truth of an idea is realized in its execution and not its theory. Hence, this idea can be daunting if you approach it without a good system to guide you. But we have a good system to help us, the Connection System. This system prevents you from creating content in a vacuum that doesn't produce results or is incredibly demanding to produce.

Unfortunately, some writers do fall victim to this idea due to poor execution. Such writers often come from a journalism, academic or other traditional writing background. To them, their system involves identifying something to write (via an article assignment, book deal, etc.) and then putting their head down to research and write it. That approach is terribly inefficient and, frankly, boring because it's very isolating and lonely. In the Connection System, we flip that around.

In the Connection System, identify ways to create content while you're researching and drafting your final work. Share that content with the readers connected to your platform, listen to their responses, analyze their questions, and evolve that feedback into your continued research and writing process. By flipping the approach as we have, you not only benefit from having many more opportunities of producing valuable content for your audience but also enjoy the validation or invalidation of your ideas from your readers. This reader engagement helps you manage and tweak your ideas toward the best possible final product.

Randi Epstein is an excellent example of an author benefiting from using the Connection System to great effect. As she started researching her next book on the science and history of sex hormones and therapy, she used her blog to share the interesting facts and insights she discovered along the way. For example, she was recently invited to an embryology lab and witnessed the process of Intracytoplasmic Sperm Injection, the process of injecting a single sperm into an egg. She shared that story on her blog. She also shared great stories from her time interviewing vitro fertilization doctors at the forefront of scientific advancements in sex hormones. These stories allow her readers to share in her adventure as she's learning amazing new things. They're also the exact content she needs to further grow her community of readers and excite them about her new book before it's even published.

Creating content using this approach does take work, but it's not a second fulltime job. At most, the extra level of effort is only 20% above what you're doing already. How can that be? Because when you develop content that is adventure-driven, shares stories, mirrors DVD extras and, generally, re-images great content you've already made, your content takes on the qualities of a shared network where each element overlaps and supports another. This works so well because it drastically reduces the amount of time and energy required from you as well as adding structure and support to your entire platform.

- CREATING FLAGSHIP CONTENT -

Chris Guillebeau is the bestselling author of *The Art of Non-Conformity* and *The $100 Startup*. Those successful books were propelled by Chris' incredibly engaged platform, which rallies at ChrisGuillebeau.com. Chris has long been devoted to writing and publishing high-value content for his readers. "Flagship content" has been a key to his strategy, which he describes in his popular free ebook *279 Days to Overnight Success*, a shining example of flagship content itself.

Flagship content is any substantial piece of writing that can stand on its own, conveys a strong set of principles and is created and published in such a way as to encourage rapid sharing. In Chris' case, he made his ebook into an easy to read, well-designed PDF that readers could download from his site with one click.

279 Days to Overnight Success wasn't Chris' first influential ebook. When he was just getting started he spent several weeks writing his manifesto *A Brief Guide to World Domination*, which outlines the core principles of his tribe along with his goals and an invitation for people to join him. That manifesto has been downloaded over 100,000 times, a classic example of how flagship content can help launch and fuel a successful writing career for the long-term.

Manifestos and other forms of flagship content are so useful because they leave no doubt about what readers will experience if they join the tribe and subscribe to its content. This sets the proper expectations now and for the future. When you don't manage expectations properly, or don't set them at all, that's when those patched holes in your bucket start to burst open. People leave tribes when they don't understand its principles, or when those principles have been changed on them.

So, do your readers have the same level of understanding about your tribe as Chris' readers do about his? Have you worked hard to set clear expectations about what your writings are all about, and why readers should pay attention? Any author that hasn't done this has some work to do. Here are two ways to start, both focusing on creating your flagship content.

First, write your own manifesto. It doesn't need to be as long or highly produced as Chris' to be effective, though it certainly can be. The important thing is that you outline your beliefs and goals in the manifesto and make it easy to download and read. Second, do a blog post series based on your manifesto. Take tenants and core beliefs that you expressed and create a series of blog posts that explain them further. Once the entire series is complete, link to those blog posts on your about page.

Flagship content serves as the big milestones in your adventure-driven content platform. They are entry points for new readers as well as reflection points for existing readers. This makes flagship content a very special type of evergreen content.

– EVERGREEN CONTENT –

How useful is yesterday's newspaper? How about last week's newspaper, or the one from a year ago today? Is that information still relevant and valuable? Do you, as a consumer, seek out content that is outdated? Probably not because you want the most recent and relevant content you can find. Your readers are the same way; they want content from you that is current and relevant. Here's the thing: You don't always have to be cranking out fresh content every day; you just have to create content that stays fresh over time. That's evergreen content.

The opposite of evergreen content is content with a short shelf life, meaning it goes out of date quickly. If you constantly chase the latest news headline, fad or gossip story, then you're creating content that won't remain interesting or relevant for very long. Therefore, you'll need to create a lot of new content very frequently simply to keep up with what's trending. That's a hamster wheel approach to content creation that is never-ending. That's not a fun place to be and quickly becomes overwhelming. Instead, focus on creating content that will stand the test of time.

My business coach always reminds me of that important lesson. "When in doubt, create assets," he says. And he's right. Evergreen content is an asset, and a really important one, because it continues to work and deliver value while you sleep. Chris Guillebeau's manifestos increase his audience size all by themselves; he doesn't have to do anything anymore. They're available and constantly attracting attention from the right readers for his tribe. So, don't create something just because you think it'll be popular. Focus on creating assets that will add value to your readers long into the future.

- A WORD ON ANALYTICS -

As with everything in this book, we want to focus all of our energy on the things that work and strip away the things that don't. Therefore, in order to make sure your content is making a difference, you need to track how it's working. That means you'll have to spend some time getting comfortable with analytics.

There are a lot of tools available to track your website analytics. Most of them offer the same core set of features. Here are the things you want to track on your website:

- **Number of visitors.** How many people are coming to your website on a weekly or monthly basis? And is that number growing or shrinking over time?

- **Number of pageviews.** How many total pages on your site are being visited? And is that number also growing or shrinking?

- **Popular pages.** Which pages on your website are being visited the most? This will help you see what your fans are interested in reading as you think about creating new content in the future, whether free content or books.

- **Referrers.** Which websites are linking to your site, and how many people are they sending? When you see other sites linking to you, that's a great time to reach out and build connections with their creators, writers or editors.

Of course, much more data exists inside your analytics tool, but these four statistics will allow you to keep an eye on how your site is growing, where traffic is coming from and what content people are paying attention to the most. As with any technology, I prefer to share my latest thoughts online so that I can easily update them as the technologies change. To see my latest recommendation for an analytics tool along with a download of the stats spreadsheet I use with my clients, visit www.first1000copies.com/analytics.

– CONTENT –

By now, the value of remarkable content to your author platform should be very clear. Permission is great to have, but if you don't consistently deliver adventure-driven, story-focused, fan-centric, evergreen content then you risk losing that permission. Without such content, your readers won't have anything they can easily engage with or share. If they can't engage or share your content, then your whole Connection System stops functioning the way it should.

Remember that relationships are at the center of the Connection System. Relationships require care and feeding to stay healthy and active. This relationship building through content is what keeps readers interested in your ideas, which naturally leads to book sales.

CHAPTER TAKEAWAYS

. . . .

Error on the side of sharing too much.

. . . .

Obscurity is the most dangerous thing for authors.

. . . .

Treat your writing career as an adventure and use your blog to share that adventure.

. . . .

Learn how to re-imagine what you're already created into other forms of content.

. . . .

Create content that will stand the test of time.

. . . .

Keep track of the right analytics about your content so you can see how it's working.

- OUTREACH -

Permission is at the heart of the Connection System. Content gives that heart a rhythm, pumping life into your platform. By themselves, permission and content are enough to do an okay job managing and growing your platform. But bestselling authors don't settle for good enough. They didn't become bestselling authors by stopping there; instead, they pushed forward through outreach. Outreach takes your sturdy platform and makes is stronger by expanding its influence. And when you're in competition for attention in today's attention deprived world (all authors are), smart outreach efforts can make all the difference.

Without a dedicated outreach plan, your platform will grow but at a slow pace. People will trickle in after they've discovered you through a Google search or a random piece of word-of-mouth. Of course, we don't want to build a system to only grow at a snail's pace. We want to build a system that expands like wildfire. You cannot harness that wildfire into your bucket if you don't already have your permission and content elements in place. But when you do, it's time to shift up a gear and get noticed.

Let's take a moment to remember the goal of the Connection System: to create a system that allows you to connect with new readers in a way that naturally leads to selling more books. Outreach is a fundamental part of this system because it keeps the cycle moving. Without outreach efforts, your content isn't effectively growing your permission assets like your email list, which hinders how many books you sell. That may seem obvious, but I see so many authors make the mistake of devaluing its importance for their platform, an error that wastes time and alienates potential fans. The mistakes usually start when authors approach outreach with the wrong attitude and motivation. So that's where we'll start our exploration of outreach: the attitude and motivation that empower bestselling authors to share their message as wide and far as possible to grow their platform to its full potential. If you get this part wrong, you'll find yourself alienated from the writing community and see your book sales flatline.

Once you have the right attitude and motivation, you can start extending and multiplying connections that introduce you to new readers. If you manage that outreach well, you'll save yourself enormous amounts of time while connecting with a lot of other great writers and influencers. Where do you start such an outreach plan?

You start with empathy.

- EMPATHY -

Empathy is "the intellectual identification with or vicarious experiencing of feelings, thoughts or attitudes of another."[vii] The most important part of that definition is the end: "of another." As an author, if you're not attuned to the needs and wants of your reader, and if you aren't working hard to deliver content that matches those feelings, then you're missing the mark. So, before you send that email or make that phone call pitching your book, article or blog post, take a deep breath and ask these questions:

What does she want out of life?

What stresses her out?

What could I do to make her life easier?

What is her daily job? Could I make that easier in some way?

Ultimately, how can I help her get what she wants out of life?

You've likely heard of the golden rule: treat people how you want to be treated. That's the essence of empathy, which the car salesman from the earlier story completely forgot. He was trying to get me to buy the latest model of his minivan, a result that was not aligned to my best interest. That's why he failed to leave a positive impression, and why I'll never interact with him again.

This mismatching of attitude and best interest is where I see so many authors make fundamental mistakes, especially at the beginning of their careers. Many are so desperate to sell books that they become completely focused on themselves. Thus, when they start to work with other people, they think only of their own goals. This attitude isn't appreciated and is very isolating. So always approach outreach opportunities by first putting yourself in the other person's shoes. Then look for ways where you can overlap your interests with theirs, thereby creating a win-win situation that everyone can enjoy.

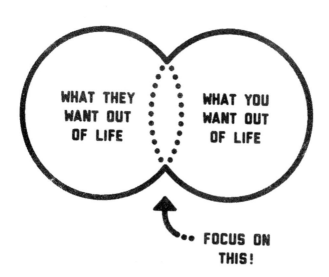

- HELP FIRST -

"You can get everything you want in life if you just help enough other people get what they want in life." Zig Ziglar, famous motivational speaker and author, gave that advice throughout his legendary career. This advice symbolizes the idea behind using outreach efforts to build relationships through empathy. It's the most powerful and effective approach possible. It's also not an overnight solution. So, before we proceed any further, ask yourself this question:

"Do I want to be someone who wrote a book once, or do I want to be someone with a writing career?"

Long-term career plans require long-term thinking. Writers with shortsighted attitudes fail to grasp this model, which is why many writing careers fizzle out after just one book. Thankfully, our model is rooted in the new definition of marketing: the act of building long-lasting connections with people. This idea can only become a reality if you help others get what they want out of life.

- TWO EMAILS -

Two authors recently emailed me for the first time. The subject line of the first read, "Let's meet." The email shared the author's struggle marketing his book and a request for a phone call so he could "pick my brain" about what he was doing wrong and how to fix it.

The subject line of the second email read, "Interview." The email was a request to interview me for his podcast so that he could share my advice to help educate his listeners and promote my business.

Which one do you think got a response from me?

Both of these authors were after the same thing but approached the opportunity from the opposite perspective. Context matters. The context of the first email conveyed selfishness. The context of the second email conveyed service. Service adds value to the world because it is born of an abundance attitude. Selfishness, at best, neither adds nor subtracts value from the world because it is born of a scarcity attitude. Choose to see and interact with the world through the perspective of abundance and you'll soon experience that abundance too.

- MAKE MY LIFE EASIER -

I cut my Internet marketing teeth in the early days of blogging by starting a blog network in the cycling industry. Pretty soon, I was on all of the hit lists for publicists about new products in the industry.

One of those publicists was a small publishing imprint that only released books about cycling. They constantly wanted to send me their latest book to read and review on one of our blogs. I appreciated their interest, but there was a problem: I was busy. I had a lot going on managing the network, which included producing content all day, every day. Reviewing a book only added to that workload because I would have to spend several hours reading the book, thinking through my reaction, deciding on a writing angle and, finally, writing it.

When pitches from publicists like this arrived, I almost always said no because the effort just wasn't worth it.

But then, one time, an author of a new cycling book approached me by asking if he could write something for one of my blogs. His idea was to write an article containing helpful tips for how cyclists can stay safe while riding at night. The advice was based on his book.

Here again, two different people after the same goal. This time, one person asked for 4 to 5 hours of my time. The other offered to save me time. Which one do you think got a response from me and had the chance to have their book featured?

Little mistakes like these are a big deal when trying to build an effective outreach plan. In most cases, these mistakes are unintentional. Instead of learning from them, the average person repeats them because she doesn't consistently check her assumptions.

- ASSUMPTIONS -

Assumptions can be helpful or harmful. The good ones motivate you to think critically and act with empathy. The bad ones trick you into thinking rashly and acting selfishly. When you're ready to launch into your outreach plan, make sure you have these assumptions in check.

- Assume other people are busier than you.

- Assume that everyone's default behavior is to protect his or her time and workload, and that's ok.

- Assume that if they say "no" that it's for a very good, legitimate reason.

- Assume that if they ignore you that it's for a very good, legitimate reason.

- Assume that if they say "yes" that you have one chance to follow through on making their life easier.

When you are in outreach mode, revoke your right to be offended. You're not always going to get the answer you want. People are going to turn you down or just ignore you from time to time. That's a part of the game; that's a part of life. When you don't get a favorable response, take a breath and move forward. Keep looking for ways to help other people. Always assume the best of people. Success comes through persistence because everything operates on the law of averages. You simply have to try enough times to produce the results you want.

- FANS AND INFLUENCERS -

Successful authors understand the distinction between fans and influencers, and target them both with their outreach efforts. Building long-lasting connections with both groups is very important to keep the Connection System cycle flowing.

Fans are people that will buy your book. She is someone for whom your writing makes a direct and positive impact in her life. Because your work is so helpful to her, she wants to get to know you better and stay connected with your latest writings. And she'll continue recommending your books to her family and friends.

By contrast, influencers are people that will get other people to buy your book.

The widely read blogger that recommends your book to all of his readers is an influencer.

The popular reviewer on Goodreads, the social platform that helps readers find and share books they love, with a large following is an influencer.

The writer with a large email list is an influencer.

The person booking guests for the local radio show is an influencer. He has built his own Connection System in which people enjoy his content and trust his judgment. So when he says that your book is interesting and helpful, then they're likely to buy it.

You need to interact with these two groups in different ways because they have distinct needs and communication expectations. Fans want relentlessly helpful content from you on a regular basis. Due to that volume of content and the nature of their engagement (via an email list or other subscription platform), you need to use one-to-many communication: blogs, email newsletters, social media, etc. Influencers, however, likely don't want to receive every piece of your content because they're just as busy as you are producing content. Even if they're your good friends, influencers won't want to receive as many one-to-many communications as fans do. Thus, when you are engaging influencers, always use one-to-one communication: phone calls, email, coffee meetups, etc.

For both groups, the goal is to help them get what they want out of life. For fans, you're helping by delivering on the promise of high quality content on a regular basis as well as personal interactions and insights. For influencers, you're helping by giving them ready-to-go content they can share with their audience, which they appreciate because it saves them time while still giving value to their audience.

Linking communities together in this fashion creates a wonderful win-win-win effect. Your platform grows as more readers discover you and learn about your work. Your fans enjoy being a part of a thriving community with diverse influences from other communities. And the influencers of those other communities welcome helping a fellow author like you in a way that also adds value to their audience.

All this cross-community connection building relies on the empathy, helpfulness and assumptions we established earlier. Without these attitudes and motivations in place, no amount of tactics will help you effectively persuade influencers to help you in return or convince their fans that your writing is worth following. So, if you want to avoid years of heartache and wasted effort, start building long-lasting connections built on trust and shared interests. To do that well, you must become friendly with other platforms.

- OTHER PLATFORMS -

Speaking only to your platform isn't going to help you spread your message quickly, especially when you're first starting out. However, if you get invited to be a part of other established platforms, your name and ideas will be recognized fast and travel faster. That's the most effective way to build your own platform: introduce yourself to existing platforms.

So, if you write fantasy romance novels and you want to build your tribe full of fans that adore that genre, what is the most efficient way to do it? Inviting them to your platform one-by-one as you meet them? Replying to people one at a time on Twitter that mention anything about romance novels? Neither. The best way is to show up where those fans are already congregating and share a bit about your stories and characters.

To successfully recruit fans of other platforms to join yours as well, there are three steps you must follow:

1. **Profile your readers.** What do they believe? What do they enjoy? What else do they read? Are they male or female? What is their age bracket? What kind of income do they make? Answer these questions allows you to clearly image your ideal reader. Odds are you've already done this without thinking about it. Close your eyes and picture someone reading your book. Is it a 45-year-old female or an 18-year-old boy? Does she attend plays or watch reality television? Would he feel more comfortable at Burning Man or Broadway?

2. **Identify where they spend their time.** Where are you most likely to find the type of person you just described in step one? Do they attend conferences? Do they form book clubs? Do they gather in online forums? What blogs and websites do they read? Who are their friends? Who are their influencers? Do they favor per-

sonal networks or professional networks?

3. Create an introduction approach to this platform(s).
Could you speak at the conference? Could you give a discount to the book club? Could you participate in online discussions? Could you write a guest post for the blog? Could you facilitate an interactive chat session? Could you sponsor the event? Could you interview the platform's creator?

Others have already invested the time and effort to build platforms around the same theme that you care about and support with your work. At the least, you should engage these other platforms as a fan. But don't overlook the opportunities to introduce yourself to them as a writer able and willing to contribute to them in a big way by sharing your work.

- SOCIAL MEDIA -

When I was a kid, my dad had me help him work on the cars or around the house. Back then, I always thought he couldn't do the work without me. Of course now, in retrospect, I know having me around was less about how much help I was and more about teaching me a few life lessons. During those experiences, I learned pretty quickly how to use the common tools: the hammer, screwdriver, tape measure, saw, etc. But from time to time I would come across a tool that, no matter how much a studied it, I could not figure out what it was for or the proper way to use it. Social media is like this in our age of digital outreach tools.

Social media seems important; everyone else seems to be using it with great success. But no matter how much we study it or try to use it, we are often left confused and frustrated by it because the results don't seem to match the amount of effort we put into it. A big reason for this confusion is the constantly shifting social media landscape.

As I write this, Facebook is preparing another major overhaul that will fundamentally change how we interact with it. Over the last year, Pinterest has exploded onto the scene as a major contender in the social media space. Ironically, marketers are still trying to figure out what to do with it. People have turned to Twitter to get the latest news and information, but any kind of direct promotion seems to fall short of expectations for conversion and sales. Given this climate of rapid change and inconsistent results, what are we to think of social media as a useful tool in our Connection System toolbox?

From my work with and study of authors, I think we must now regard social media mostly as a Connection System booster and not a Connection System driver. It's the extra cherry on top. Social media by its nature cannot establish permission and nurture trust like other platforms. Social media by its nature does not itself embody high value, evergreen content. And social media by its nature does not allow for the exchange of as much empathy or helpfulness as other forms of connections. Unfortunately, many people look to social media platforms to produce results they were never inherently built to produce. That disconnect creates endless confusion and frustration.

Bottom-line: Social media can make an author platform stronger by giving it a boost when it's already built and functioning. But social media alone cannot make an author platform strong. Bestselling authors use social media to extend their outreach plan, not to represent all of it. They use social media to support and complement their core assets: their email list, their blog, their guest posts, their outreach. So, as you further your ideas about outreach, remember that social media is a support tool only. If used unwisely, you'll end up wasting huge amounts of time.

- BUSINESS VERSUS PLEASURE -

Despite my cautions about social media, I actually really like it. Social media is fun because it is built upon the idea of personal connections. Facebook allows me to connect with old friends as well as see pictures of my nieces and nephew that live on the other side of the country. Twitter allows me to follow individuals and companies I admire and learn from what they share. Pinterest allows me to visually experience a treasure trove of inspiration from artists and brands that matter to me. All of this personal interaction brings me great pleasure. All of it can also be a huge distraction from the important work that I have to do for my author clients and for my business at large. So where do we draw the line between business and pleasure? We're about to find out.

- WHAT IS IT FOR? -

The Connection System is made up of four important phases: Permission, Content, Outreach and Sell. These phases work together in a natural cycle to allow you to interact with readers and create long-lasting connections that will get people excited about buying your books. Social media is not a useful tool in all of those phases because it is not a reliable way of compelling your followers to take action. Specifically, it's not a valuable Content tool because, although it is a way to share content, it's not intended to share large amounts of original content. Your email list is far better suited for that. And because story-driven, evergreen content is more persuasive than any other form of content, your email list or website is a much better choice.

For example, one of my author clients has over 200,000 followers on Twitter. We marketed his new book to his Twitter followers at the same time we marketed it to his email list. The social media results were poor. In fact, for every one book we sold through social media, we sold over ten books through his email list. I've validated these results across many different authors. In every instance, selling through social media dramatically underperforms selling through email lists. Consequently, authors that focus on social media as a part of their Sell strategy aren't as successful as those that only use social media for Outreach.

Social media offers value as an Outreach tool because it allows you to establish connections with new people and engage in public conversation. Such engagement provides the "booster" effect that can make your platform's overall results a little bit better. But that's where social media stops being a useful business tool. Anything beyond that risks wasting time trying to use it in ways it was not intended.

- SOCIAL MEDIA FOR INTRODUCTION AND INVITATION -

When you see that social media is best used as a booster engine to your platform, you'll discover that those little boosts are best sparked by small bits and pieces of content that don't fit into other parts of your platform. Creative thoughts, inspiring quotes and special moments are all great things to share on social media. They allow you to quickly add little tidbits of value to your readers as you come across them.

Gretchen Rubin, *New York Times* bestselling author of *The Happiness Project* and *Happier at Home*, uses her Facebook page in exactly this way. She shares tidbits of ideas that aren't robust enough to make into a featured blog post or full email newsletter. By posting these tidbits to her Facebook page, she's inviting her readers to join in her adventures as a writer. That's precisely what outreach is all about: boosting the connections with readers. It's not about selling, which she confirmed when I questioned her about the usefulness of Facebook in selling books. Her response needs no interpretation:

"Because Facebook changes all the time, I try to get them to sign up for a list, or become blog-readers, because that's a more direct connection, but I meet them on Facebook. [...] I always look for chances to encourage readers to sign up for something or request something. That kind of back-and-forth is the way to build a reader-writer relationship (it seems to me). So Facebook gives me a chance to keep people interested in my writing, and also make them aware of other things that they might enjoy that I can give them."

Facebook, and other social media, can be a way to boost engagement with readers but should be viewed as the spark, not the driver, of the relationship. Always look for ways to invite people to go deeper with you and your content. Little sparks can help a lot to achieve this goal, but they can't replace the need to do the fundamental platform-building work well.

- MAKE IT EASY TO SHARE YOUR STUFF -

The booster power of social media is rooted in connections with a lot of people. Billions of people use these channels every day to stay connected. These connections are what make social media a useful tool for you to introduce yourself to new people. But that usefulness is only possible if you make it easy to share what work you're doing.

For example, when you put content on your website, whether it's a new blog post or downloadable manifesto, have buttons available to share that content with just one click of the mouse. Additionally, create pre-written 120 character takeaways (so there is room in the allowable 140 characters to add something of their own) that people can immediately copy and paste into a Twitter update.

You should also focus on making your social media content visual. Images generate far more Facebook Likes than any other content shared on Facebook.[viii] Images are very popular on Twitter too.[ix] And Pinterest is built entirely on images. The Facebook page *I Fucking Love Science* built up over 4 million likes in just a year of existence by relying heavily on images for their content. Highly clickable headlines are equally important.[x] Newspapers have long relied on the headline of their cover story to drive sales. The logic is the same for social media: People have a fraction of a second to decide whether or not they'll read your content. Make it easy for them to decide in favor of your content.

- DON'T FOCUS ON NUMBERS -

Focusing solely on numbers is the second major social media pitfall. Many authors fall into this trap because it's so easy to see how many people have liked your Facebook page or are following you on Twitter. When these numbers become your focus, your efforts shift from creating long-lasting connections with readers to doing anything you can to inflate your numbers. Some authors start following anyone on Twitter hoping that they'll follow them back. Others constantly push their Facebook page on everyone hoping they'll click the Like button.

What good does this do? Does this strengthen their reader connections? Does this increase book sales? Does this gain more respect from influencers? No. Artificially driving up social media numbers does nothing to help any author achieve his or her most important platform goal: creating long-lasting connections with readers by being relentlessly helpful. So don't get caught up in the numbers game. And choose your social media carefully.

- PICK YOUR SOCIAL MEDIA CAREFULLY -

Social media platforms aren't all created equal. Some work in similar ways. Some look the same. But who uses these platforms and why can vary greatly, as can the population sizes of those platforms. How many people are on Google+ that aren't on Twitter? How many people are on Twitter that aren't on Facebook? What type of people use Facebook instead of Twitter? Is your audience more likely to be on Pinterest or Facebook? What kind of content is shared most on these platforms, and how does that kind of content match the interests of your readers?

Mainstream marketing advice suggests that you must jump on every new social platform that pops up or risk missing out on some major benefit. But what would you really be missing except extra commitments of your time that likely don't result in more book sales? And because social media is so fickle, where should you spend your limited time on social media?

To help you narrow down your options to the best for your

audience, go through the same exercise I outlined in the "Other platforms" section above. Create a profile of your ideal reader and then find out what forms of social media he or she is using. You may discover that your ideal reader isn't using social media much at all. That's perfectly fine if that's truth. Don't force social media into your strategy if it doesn't belong. Regardless, the same advice applies for any kind of outreach, social media or otherwise: The way to build your own platform is to identify other platforms where potential readers already congregate and introduce yourself there.

- LIVING WITH SOCIAL MEDIA -

Social media is in constant flux and, as a result, is often a source of frustration for authors. So far, we've looked at the major social media pitfalls that many authors fall into and how to avoid them. We've also seen how to carefully select and use social media in ways that actually benefit your author platform by delivering value to your readers. It can all be a bit confusing, so we should review the key guidelines to using social media in your Connection System:

- Don't rely on social media to establish or nurture Permission to directly and reliably communicate with your readers.

- Don't rely on social media to directly sell books.

- Understand the difference between using social media for business versus pleasure. Be honest with yourself so that you don't waste time.

- Use social media to share smaller tidbits of content that don't fit into the rest of your platform and that can boost your overall outreach efforts.

- Make it easy for people to share your content on social media.

- Focus on engaging with new people through social media instead of inflating your social media numbers.

- Don't spread yourself thin by trying to use every social media platform. Carefully choose the one or two that align best with your audience.

Authors contact me regularly asking for help with their social media strategy. What they really want help with is their overall platform strategy, even if they don't state it in those terms. They think social media and nothing else equals outreach, and that social media is also the solution to their need to produce content and sell books. Once we begin talking, however, these authors quickly realize that social media is just one small piece of their overall strategy. Bestselling authors know that social media is simply a booster to their hard work in other areas, which makes their results a little bit better. That's the art of smart author marketing.

- THE CURIOUS CASE OF AUTHOR MARKETING -

Marketing is an interesting animal. There is huge diversity in how authors market their books. Although the fundamentals are the same, everyone has their own approach so that their platform is unique. Individuals and companies in other industries do something similar so that they can compete against one another. Apple versus Google is a classic example. And I'm a perfect case study.

I'm an Apple enthusiast. I'm writing this book on my iMac with my iPhone and iPad sitting next to it on my desk. Apple competes directly with Google on smartphones. The interesting thing about being an Apple enthusiast is that, thanks to my general Apple loyalty, I am immediately disinterested in anything Google offers that is Android related. This kind of all-or-nothing loyalty, however, isn't the case with authors.

Author marketing is peculiar because it generally lacks competition between authors. In fact, taking the glass-half-full mentality, there are huge opportunities for authors to work together. Just look at the curious case of Dan Ariely. *Predictably Irrational* was Dan's first book. It became a big success very quickly because of its unique examination of behavioral economics. That subject overlaps with books from other popular authors like Dan Pink, Robert Cialdini, Ori Brafman, Daniel Gilbert, Chip and Dan Heath and others. Here's the thing: Being a fan of Dan Ariely's book makes you more likely, not less, to desire, buy and enjoy books from those other authors.

Authors have known about this effect for years. At least the bestsellers have. That's why most popular books have blurbs on their covers written by other successful authors. They're cross-marketing each other's books because anytime there is interaction both platforms grow.

- LIVE EVENTS -

For all the emphasis on online outreach via email and social media, the best outreach an author can do is offline in the real world. When you meet with a fan or an influencer face-to-face, it's impossible not to begin (or expand) an empathetic relationship. When you're face-to-face, you can more easily test your assumptions. And when you're face-to-face, you can discover opportunities that may never present themselves through an online conversation. And for all of those reasons, offline outreach can be scary. I know firsthand what that's like.

Shifting my company's focus to work exclusively with authors was a scary decision. At the time, I only had a handful of clients that were authors and no contacts inside the industry. What I did have, however, was a registration for the next South by Southwest (SXSW) Interactive conference in Austin, Texas. SXSW Interactive focuses on emerging technology and its amazing influence on business. Some of the best and brightest minds from all corners of the interactive world attend SXSW every year. If there was ever an event where my ideal audience was gathering, this was it.

In the lead-up to the conference, I went into a frenzy researching every speaker and found every one that had ever written a book. I then began searching Twitter and the SXSW online community for anyone that worked in the publishing industry. Once I had made my list, I began contacting every one of them asking to set up a meeting during the conference. I scheduled meetings anywhere from 6:00 a.m. to 11:00 p.m. My hard work paid off because, when I landed in Austin the day of the conference, I had a schedule packed with people in the industry, some potential clients and others key influencers.

My time at SXSW was over before I knew it. The experience was exhausting but totally worth it because I had two new clients and over a dozen new contacts by the time I got home. I had worked hard to get my business well positioned for a lot of growth within the publishing world. Those outreach efforts then continue to provide opportunities today.

Most people don't approach conferences like I did. They attend more for the content and less for the connections. Conference content is often very valuable, but it holds far less long-term value than leveraging the opportunity to build and nurture long-lasting relationships with fans and influencers. The authors that approach conferences eager to meet some of the hundreds or thousands of people that have congregated together are the ones that put themselves in the best position to build successful careers.

Writers can take advantage of conferences in two important and distinct ways:

First, conferences are often a great place to meet book agents or publishing professionals that can help you get a foothold in the industry. You need not close a deal right then and there; the idea is to build a relationship that you can leverage in the future when you're ready. Second, conferences are a wonderful way to meet your readers in person, which elevates their support of your work and increases the likelihood that they'll not only buy your next book but also share it with their friends and family.

Dan Ariely, bestselling author of *Predictably Irrational* and *The Honest Truth About Dishonesty*, has a great approach to conferences. When we started working with Dan, I asked him why he had his entire travel schedule on his website. "That way if my readers see that I'm coming to their city, I can meet them for coffee or something," he replied. Clearly, Dan understands that nothing builds a connection with fans and influencers more than meeting them face-to-face. And he understands that live events are the most efficient way to do precisely that.

If you would like my step-by-step guide to taking full advantage of live events, you can download it at www.first1000copies.com/events.

- WRITE FOR INFLUENCERS -

Scott Dinsmore's platform languished at 100 subscribers for the first four years of its existence. Then he decided to get serious. He rebranded his platform as *Live Your Legend* and gave it a single focus: connecting with influencers and providing them great content for their platforms. With this new focus, Scott began submitting guest articles to blogs and websites about entrepreneurship, happiness and living your passion. He reached out to all kinds of authors, magazines and bloggers. His outreach results were twofold.

First, he created long-lasting connections with a large group of influencers because he took the time to understand them and their audiences, and then added value by providing great content. Second, his email list experienced explosive growth. His list grew by 600% in the first six months, and then by 1600% in the following 12 months. Today, two years later, he has over 30,000 subscribers on his email list.

Scott's story reminds us that the best way to build your own platform is to introduce yourself to existing ones. Outreach to influencers in your market or genre is the ideal starting point. Always remember to deliver relentlessly helpful content that is empathetic to the needs and desires of the intended audience. And be sure to follow up that content with a bit of social media engagement to give the effect a little boost.

- DON'T LIMIT YOURSELF TO A-LISTERS -

Diversity is an important aspect to any solid outreach strategy. You never know which specific opportunity may work, or which kind of opportunity works best. Therefore, you should never put all your outreach eggs in one basket.

Unfortunately, many writers put all their outreach eggs into the A-list writer basket. Reaching out to such top-tier influencers is a good idea, but it's a risky move by itself. I know from experience that writers at that level receive a ton of guest post submissions and similar offers. Most A-listers I know are good and genuine people that want to help. But they're also human with limited time and too many incoming offers. So what should you do?

You should balance your outreach strategy with mid-tier writers and writers at your same level of platform growth. Targeting B-list writers and peers presents a lot of advantages. First, they don't get as many offers as A-list writers do, so the odds of getting a positive response are much higher. Second, they probably have more time to spend with you so you can create a deeper, longer lasting connection. Third, they need help promoting what they do far more than the A-listers, so they'll be more open to your offers.

In each outreach opportunity, focus on creating a community. By connecting with other writers and influencers that are in your same space and closer to your level, you'll get a lot more traction and you'll be able to grow together.

- A FEW THINGS NOT TO DO -

To be successful in your author career, you need to approach outreach opportunities with enthusiasm, confidence and drive. You should not, however, be an asshole.

Don't keep a quid-pro-quo list of everything you do to help people so you can immediately ask for a return on the favor.

Don't get angry when someone ignores you or turns you down.

Don't assume you're more important than other people.

Don't have unrealistic expectations of people.

Instead, embrace the golden rule: Treat people the way you want to be treated. This is the positive attitude that breeds the best results. And outreach is all about attitude because it determines your motivations. Selfish motivations are turnoffs. Selfless motivations are attractive. People want to be associated with others that are willing to give of themselves without the expectation of a reward. So, if you genuinely do something to help someone else and then later humbly ask for his or her help, you'll be much more likely to get a positive response. That's how human nature works.

- A WORD ON ANALYTICS -

While at first it may seem uncomfortable to measure relationship building, you need to make sure your efforts are getting results. Each phase of the Connection System needs to be evaluated. So far, you've learned what analytics to track for Permission and Content. Now, here are the analytics you'll want to monitor for Outreach. They should help you answer the most important question:

- **Number of new influencer connections.** Whether you meet someone at a live event or by writing a guest post, have you created a connection with that person that will allow you to stay in touch long term?

- **Engagement.** We want to focus on fans, not numbers. So, when you put something out through social media, what happens? How many people engage, share or respond?

For my latest recommendation on the right platform for outreach analytics and walkthroughs on how to track the right numbers, visit www.first1000copies.com/analytics.

- OUTREACH -

Outreach plays a vital role within the Connection System. Outreach efforts allow you to grow your platform to its full potential at a strong rate. Otherwise, your platform may grow, but slowly and not enough to really accelerate your author career.

Remember that the spirit of Outreach is inviting people to join your adventures as a writer as experienced through your books, blog posts and other forms of content. Permission is needed to make this happened. Without it, your other efforts won't be nearly as effective as they could have been. Assuming you've done a great job with the Permission and Content elements of your Connection System, then focus now on Outreach.

CHAPTER TAKEAWAYS

. . . .

First and always, help people get what they want out of life.

. . . .

Introduce yourself to existing platforms that share a common ideal reader.

. . . .

Look for ways to partner with other authors.

. . . .

Understand the difference between fans and influencers, and then engage with them appropriately.

. . . .

Use social media only as an accelerator to boost your other outreach efforts.

. . . .

Attend live events because they are great opportunities to build empathetic, lasting connections with influencers.

. . . .

Focus on long-term relationship building.

. . . .

Have fun because if you're not then you're not
doing it right.

SELL

- PLUGGED HOLES -

Permission may be the cornerstone of your Connection System. Content may be the lifeblood of your platform. And Outreach may be the big boost your marketing efforts have been looking for. But they'll all be for not if you don't finish building your Connection System with the final big piece: Selling.

The good news is that by now we've fixed the holey bucket problem that many authors experience. Through Permission, we've plugged the holes by engaging readers and creating connections with them. And through a combination of Content and Outreach, we've added more interested readers into the bucket by providing valuable content and an empathetic community. But that attraction isn't enough to move them to buy your book. Remember that the goal isn't just about growing an email list; it's about inviting your readers to purchase your books. That's what Selling is for, and this is how it starts.

- BE YOUR OWN FAN -

I recently spoke with an author about three months before his book launched. He has a very large following on his blog as well as a very active email subscriber base. Due to his audience size and its engagement level, I was curious to know what he was planning on doing to launch his book. So I asked him.

"I don't know," he said. "I'll probably do a blog post the day it comes out."

"What about your email list?" I replied.

"I wasn't planning on sending anything."

"Why not?"

"I don't want to get too salesy."

That mindset is tragic because it's misinformed. Should you be concerned about how your audience will interpret your book launch promotions? Absolutely. But the only authors that need to worry about coming across as "salesy" are those that haven't taken the time to build an authentic Connection System based on value, trust, empathy and respect. The bestselling authors I work with understand this difference. They understand that the problem is not being too salesy. The problem is lacking enthusiasm. Enthusiasm has fueled your platform already. It has energized your message, powered your content and sparked your outreach. Your readers read your writing because they are enthused by your ideas and advice. So, when it comes time to launch your book, you need to show the same level of enthusiasm. If you don't, then why should readers excite themselves?

There's an easy way to prevent a lack of enthusiasm in your selling: Be your own fan.

Your writing is good for people. You wrote a book to add value to peoples' lives. When it's time to sell your book, you have to invite people to buy it and explain why it's good for them using the same level of confidence and energy that you've put into everything else. Your enthusiasm will, more than anything else, convince them to buy. Nothing will work if you don't put your own excitement into the process.

- ASK THEM TO BUY -

With your enthusiasm in check, you have to ask for the sale. It's as simple as that. There's nothing to be ashamed of in asking to be compensated for your hard work. If the offer is fair, then everyone benefits. People trade things they have for things they want all the time. That's economics; it's normal.

Beyond asking, there aren't many other "rules" to selling. There are, however, some best practices that can make your selling efforts more effective. The first best practice is perhaps the most important: People should not be on your email list long before inviting them to buy something, even just one book.

So, by all means, tell them about your book. Let them download a sample. Explain the plot. Share how the book will help them lose weight, or meet new people, or stand a better chance of getting a promotion, or improve their business practices. Share the blurbs you got for the book. Tell them about all of the five-star reviews your book has received. Do all of those things if you can because they'll stimulate interest in your book. But interest isn't enough. At some point, you need to invite them to buy your book.

- WHET THEIR APPETITE -

Amazon makes the first 10% of their Kindle books available as a free sample. I've used such free samples to "taste test" a lot of books. In many cases, I try out the sample and get hooked enough to pay for the whole book. Amazon's logic here is simple and effective: If you read the first 10% of a book and enjoy it, the likelihood of you buying the full version goes up significantly. That's another selling best practice you should adopt.

What free sample to give away, and where, varies from author to author. As we saw with Chris Guillebeau, he offers high quality PDF books like his manifesto for free download. Others like Chip and Dan Heath give away great resources via their email newsletter. You can use the first part of your book in exactly the same way. You can create a PDF that has the full cover image, table of contents, and introduction or first chapter. In fact, since you have complete control of when the sample ends, make sure it leaves the reader at a point where they will be dying to read more. This freebie can be made available as a bonus for subscribing to your email list, a free download, even a magnet to attract outreach opportunities.

The cliffhanger is key because it sets up the one-two punch. What's the second punch that delivers the knockout? The call-to-action page. On this page, include the following items:

- Blurbs from your highest profile reviewers.

- A picture of yourself and a short biography.

- Hyperlinks to buy your book.

Make the purchase decision and buying action super easy for your reader. Don't put any barriers between them and clicking to buy. Barriers could be unnecessary images or over stylized text. And definitely don't include any other links except for your buy now link. Bottom-line: Once you have hooked your readers with the content, put them over the edge with a strong call-to-action that makes the sale.

- LEAVE THEM WANTING MORE -

Derek Halpern has mastered the "whet their appetite" best practice. At the end of his webinars, *not* clicking the buy button is almost impossible. How does he create such excitement and desire for his offer? He gives them a lot of amazing content for free while still leaving them waiting more.

Less than two years ago, Derek began SocialTriggers.com, a blog that has skyrocketed to the top of the charts in the online marketing space. He creates extremely compelling content that offers a lot of value and insight on a regular basis.

I'm a fan.

Awhile back, Derek decided to launch an online course about how to build a popular blog. As part of the launch, he held a free 45-minute webinar sharing one of his tried-and-true blog templates. He explained how it works, why it works and how you can use it on your own blog. This was fantastic, valuable content offered for free. But he also let you know that this template was just one of the seven templates available as part of his course, along with a lot more related content that went above and beyond the material covered in the webinar. Because the webinar was so valuable by itself, many of the attendees felt like they *had* to sign up for the course or they would miss out.

When you sell your book, can you create a similar experience? If you can, do it. By introducing some of your book's content in a friendly, no-risk environment, your readers will be even more willing to consider buying the full book afterwards.

- REPETITION MAKES PERFECT -

We humans rarely do anything because of a singular event. Instead, our brains need to experience a stimulus a few times before we're compelled to take an action. That behavior helps keep us safe as well as happy. It also helps us make buying decisions. Enter the next selling best practice: repetition. Whether you send your readers an email ever day, every week or every month, make sure each of those emails has a small mention or ad for your book.

How you manage this repetition is up to you. Some authors put them in the sidebar of their emails while others put them in the footer. Some include the book cover; some don't. Others use a recent book review or blurb. However you choose to include your book mention or ad, just make sure it's consistently present along with a link to where readers can buy online.

- TELL STORIES -

Stories are another powerful selling best practice, one that I have learned to appreciate and use effectively. For example, I once found myself sitting in a big conference room with beautiful mahogany furniture and high-end leather chairs. A half dozen senior managers sat around me as the CEO prepared to speak. "I have two other proposals from people that will do the work for half the price," he said. "Why should I hire you?"

Prior to working with authors, my firm helped companies of all shapes and sizes build their online presence and develop their marketing plan. This was one of those companies, but the proposal we were reviewing was unlike any other I'd written before. It was the biggest by far, and I desperately wanted to make the sale. So when the CEO told me my price was double my competitors' and asked for an explanation I started to panic.

"What answer could I possibly give to convince him to go with my firm?" Nothing came to mind so, instead, I told him a story.

"Six months ago another potential client thought we were too expensive and went with the cheaper firm. I said that was fine and let it go. Two months later they called me back, said the project was a disaster and ended up paying me more to come in, fix the problems and rebuild everything."

That did it. The CEO chuckled. I smiled and got the contract.

The lesson here is that you can only direct sell so many times before people get annoyed and start ignoring you. "Please buy my book" works, but not forever and not enough. To turn your Connection System into a true book-selling machine, you must learn to tell stories as a way to invite your readers into the selling process. Stories are familiar and stories are disarming, which means they make buying decisions more comfortable.

So, if you write business books, tell stories about companies that have made more money by implementing your practices. Or if you write weight loss books, tell stories of how people's lives have changed after dropping 25 pounds following your program. And if you write fiction, share your fan mail from readers that raves about favorite characters. If you write travel books, tell stories of people that have been to places you write about and the adventures they went on while they were there.

Regardless of what type of book you write, be sure to tell stories about how peoples' lives are better after reading your words. Do that, and more people will buy your book in the hope of experiencing the same results.

- EMOTIONALLY CONNECT WITH YOUR READERS -

Patti Digh's fan base at 37days.com is the most passionate audience I've ever seen. Her fans are diehards that interact with almost every piece of content she shares and every project she launches. When she comes out with a new book, they buy.

What Patti does better than anyone else is a best practice born from telling stories; she includes her readers *into* the story. She accomplishes that through art. Every book she writes is filled with art, and every piece of that artwork comes from her readers. Every time she works on a new book, she invites readers to submit art that resonates with the theme of the book. The art pieces that align the best make it into the book with full credit to the respective fan. And to keep that level of engagement going between books, she changes the header art on her site every month to feature a piece of fan artwork.

Image if that were you. Imagine that you took the time and effort to make a piece of art that really mattered to you. You then shared that artwork with someone you respect and enjoy following. How would you feel if that artwork showed up in a book published by that same person? Would you tell people about the book? Would you be emotionally connected to the final product? How could you not be, right?

Your books may not lend themselves to reader artwork. If that's the case, what else can you do to bring your readers into the story so that they'll be emotionally connected to the final product? Can you ask for their stories and experiences to include in the book? Can you let them name some of the characters? Could they help choose the cover design?

The best forms of selling don't feel like selling at all. When you can include fans into your story, they will no longer feel like they're being sold to but rather partnered with. Thus, they'll have a vested interest in the final product. They'll buy a copy for themselves and one for their friends too.

- WHAT HAPPENS AFTER THEY SIGN UP? -

Imagine you're at a party standing with a friend discussing the latest movie by Christopher Nolan, director of the recent Batman movies, Inception and other blockbusters. After a few minutes trading thoughts about other great directors, you've begun a friendly debate about whether or not Nolan is the greatest living movie director.

At about this time, a mutual friend walks up to join the conversation. What would you do? Would you say hello and then immediately continue the conversation where you left off? Or would you stop and say, "Hey. We're talking about the latest Christopher Nolan movie and whether or not it solidifies him as the greatest living movie director. I, of course, think it does and he," gesturing to your friend, "does not. What do you think?" Most people would choose the second choice because it's the polite option.

When new readers sign up for your email list, you need to extend this same courtesy. They probably don't know much about you and the books you've written because they've just discovered you. So the polite and prudent thing to do is to make sure everyone that signs up for your email list gets up-to-date quickly on who you are and what you do so they can easily join into future conversations.

This best practice is a very soft form of selling that is commonly handled with an email auto-responder.

- AUTO-RESPONDERS -

Gene Kim's email auto-responders are incredibly consistent and effective. When you sign up for Gene's email newsletter at his site IT Revolution, you start receiving weekly emails introducing you to all of the IT Revolution projects. Each email contains links to some of Gene's favorite posts on their blog. His readers love the emails and frequently tell him so by sharing how much value they gained from his writing.

What his readers probably don't know, however, is that Gene and I wrote those emails weeks or months before they were ever sent. We designed that auto-responder campaign to ensure that when someone signs up for his newsletter, he or she receives an email that introduces Gene and IT Revolution as well as delivers a free PDF download. After a few days, the email system automatically sends out the second email in the series. The third email fires a few days after that. This routine continues until the auto-responder campaign is out of emails.

How does this system help Gene?

It helps by providing a clear and consistent experience for everyone who joins his platform. No matter where a new reader comes from—a featured outreach article, a random Google search, or word-of-mouth referral—he or she meets Gene in precisely the same way as everyone else. Such consistency is a great asset in the selling process because it cures the most common sales killer: confusion.

Just like the person joining their friends in mid-conversation, new email subscribers won't have the same level of understanding about Gene's work as his existing readers do. His auto-responder series balances the playing field, allowing him to get his new subscribers up to date on everything so that when he sends future newsletters they won't be confused. That's a polite gesture that happens to help sell books, especially books on your backlist.

– SELLING YOUR BACKLIST BOOKS –

An author's backlist is the collection of books he or she has already written, published and marketed. This backlist is one of the most powerful assets the author has because it attracts sales long into the future without much additional effort from the author. And a great way to continue driving those sales is by featuring backlist books in your auto-responder series. Successful authors use this selling strategy because it naturally fits with the primary need of new email subscribers: they want to learn more about you. And where best to turn to learn about your work than your past books.

Even if you don't have a backlist of books yet, use an auto-responder series to get people excited about your current book project. You can use the auto-responder emails to share any of that great content you've been collecting that we discussed in the Content section. You can also use the auto-responder emails to engage your readers with questions that can help you learn more about them. In any case, use your email list to gain permission from your readers, which is the essential first step in preparing to ask them for a sale.

- A NOTE ON SELLING -

I was ready to buy Daniel Pink's next book before he was even done telling me about it. There was just one problem: his next book *To Sell Is Human* hadn't been released yet. In fact, it hadn't even been fully written. Even though I'd have to wait, I was already sold.

A full year before *To Sell Is Human* went on sale, I was sitting across from Daniel at his dinner table listening to his book pitch. The more he spoke about it the more animated he became, his hands waving in the air. I was fascinated by the subject and wanted to know more, so I kept probing him with questions, which only flamed his enthusiasm. By the end of the conversation, I couldn't wait to read it even though I had at least nine months to wait. And although I'd get an advanced copy, I was committed to buying a few. I cared that much, because Daniel cared that much. Thanks largely to his enthusiasm, I didn't feel "sold" on his book.

You'll remember that a lack of enthusiasm is one of the top mistakes authors make when attempting to sell their books. Unfortunately, I see this time and again when working with and studying authors from all genres. In fact, I once met an author that refused to autograph a copy of his book when a fan asked for it because he felt uncomfortable about that level of status.

If you aren't willing to show your enthusiasm about your book, who is?

Readers engage with your books, auto-responders, and blog posts because they care about what you're doing. If you don't reciprocate the same level of enthusiasm, then your platform's attractive shine will fade. If you're serious about preventing that from happening, then work hard to open up about what drives you. Tell them why you love your projects. Tell them why your work matters. Tell them why they'll be better off for having read your work.

Enthusiasm sells. Let it out.

- A WORD ON ANALYTICS -

Selling isn't only about qualitative enthusiasm and the willingness to ask for a sale. Selling is very much a matter of numbers. As we've seen in the three other major sections of this book, analytics play an important part in your Connection System. We've kept a consistent focus on the essential statistics you need to track. When we apply that same focus to selling, there is but one statistic worth measuring: total book sales.

If your outreach is working, more people will be visiting your website and interacting with your content. If your content is working, more people will be signing up for your email list. If your email list is working, more people will be buying your books. Those are hardcore numbers worth knowing and monitoring. For the latest way to track your analytics, including the spreadsheet I use to track them, visit www.first1000copies.com/analytics.

- SELL -

If you want to sell your books, you have to ask people to buy. And you have to be enthusiastic when you ask. You have to believe that you're being relentlessly helpful in every area of your platform, and that the offer to buy is a fair and honest part of that system. If you don't believe in that—if you're willing to seek permission, share content and engage in outreach, but not sell—then your Connection

System will never support you as you strive to become a successful author with a rewarding writing career. The Connection System only works when all of its parts work as one. That includes selling; there's no avoiding it.

The good news is that selling is fun, when done right. When you're selling to people you've built strong, long-lasting connections with, the sale is smooth and appreciated. People want the content that you're offering in your books. Embrace that opportunity.

CHAPTER TAKEAWAYS

. . . .

Be your own fan. If you're not enthusiastic, who will be?

. . . .

Give readers a great preview of your work.

. . . .

Make it easy to buy your book. Put links in every email.

. . . .

Tell great stories.

. . . .

Use auto-responders to introduce new subscribers to your body of work.

. . . .

Ask them to buy.

BUILDING THE SYSTEM

As I write this final section, I'm excited for you. I'm excited that you're going to join the ranks of writers that are building effective platforms capable of finding success in today's publishing marketplace. And with that success, you'll be able to experience the best that a modern writing career has to offer, just like some of the authors we met in this book.

Josh Kaufman gets to spend more time with his daughter while still being a successful author. Pamela Slim is writing a book that already had an audience before she penned the first word. Hugh Howey can't write fast enough to keep up with the demand of his readers. Gene Kim is selling thousands of copies of his self-published book every month.

These authors aren't outliers. They're not people with secret or insider information about the publishing industry. They're just normal people that wanted to share their stories and ideas with the world and began using the tools available to build a system that allows them to connect with readers.

The design of that system is everything. Some systems work better than others. In this book, we explored the Connection System: the process and plans I've seen hundreds of authors use to build platforms that produce results. You can have the same results, so long as you're willing to work hard for them. If you are, then now is the time to get started building your very own **Connection System**. Just imagine what's possible if you do. Selling your first 1,000 copies? That's just the beginning.

AFTERWORD

This book provides a step-by-step plan for building a Connection System to fuel your platform, connect with readers and sell more books. There's a lot of information in these pages. To help you execute on this information, I created several checklists, worksheets and related resources available for free at www.first1000copies.com. Download these if you're serious about applying what you learned in this book.

I also recommend that you get started right away. Building a Connection System is a learning process. The sooner you begin, the faster you'll develop and the more connections you'll make. I'm here to help. Please share your ideas, feedback and questions by emailing me at tim@first1000copies.com.

Your first 1,000 book sales are waiting. Go get them.

ACKNOWLEDGEMENTS AND CREDITS

My wonderful wife Candace has done nothing but encourage and support me to blaze my own trail. Without her faith in me I have no doubt that I would be sitting in a soul-crushing cubicle somewhere.

I'm so thankful for my Mom and Dad who always assumed I could do whatever I put my mind to.

This book would not exist without my clients. I can't imagine ever working with a better group of people. I learned something new from every one of them. Thanks to Ramit Sethi, Hugh MacLeod, Daniel Pink, Pamela Slim, Hugh Howey, Robert Cooper, Guy Kawasaki, Annie Murphy Paul, Barbara Corcoran, Barry Ritholtz, Cliff Atkinson, Carl Richards, Michael Bungay Stanier, John Moore, Sunni Brown, Charles Duhigg, Dan Heath, Chip Heath, Dan Ariely, Emily Bazelon, Fred Kempe, Pamela Meyer, Garret Kramer, Gene Kim, Helaine Olen, Matt Walker, Karen Hough, Marilee Adams, Kim Aubry, Jackie Huba, Jean Chatzky, Jeff Selingo, Jeff Towson, Jennifer Robin, Michael Burchell, Jessica Hagy, John Chen, Keith Streckenbach, John Durant, Joshua Waldman, Karen House, Kate White, Kayt Sukel, Kevin Pho, Lisa DiMona, Jay Moran, Jeffrey Cohn, Logan Loomis, Karissa Glanville, Manisha Thakor, Tom Fishburne, Jessica Freedman, Jayme Johnson, Michael Port, Michele Cerza, Michelle Segar, Greg Hottinger, Michael Scholtz, Patti Digh, Paul Raeburn, Fredrik Arnander, Dan Portnoy, Rachel Swarns, Rahaf Harfoush, Randi Epstein, Richard Weylman, Jim Bolton, Robert Kurson, Rohit Bhargava, Ron Lieber, Scott Ginsberg, Shawn Hunter, Westley Overcash, Anita Campbell, Linda Stout, Stephen Denny, Jeffrey Walker, Jennifer Mc-Crea, Debbie Weil, Noel Yeatts, Andrea Reiser, Todd Sattersten and Tom Shadyac.

My work life would be empty without my Out:think cohorts, Joseph Hinson and Lauren Baker—the best people in the business.

Gene Kim and Joshua Waldman were the two people that really pushed me to get this book out into the world. This book would still be an incomplete draft without them.

The people that suffered through early drafts of this book and were kind of enough to give feedback were Ishita Gupta, Carl Richards, Colleen Wainwright, Jill Murphy, Garret Kramer, Joshua Waldman, Gene Kim, Debbie Reber, Todd Sattersten, William Hertling, Dan Portnoy and Josh Kaufman.

My editor, Matt Gartland, worked overtime with me to make sure this book made sense.

Dan Portnoy is the best friend and encourager a guy could have.

ENDNOTES

I. http://dictionary.reference.com/browse/marketing?s=t

II. http://blog.twitter.com/2011/06/200-million-tweets-per-day.html

III. http://www.digitalbuzzblog.com/facebook-statistics-stats-facts-2011/

IV. http://business.ftc.gov/documents/bus61-can-spam-act-compliance-guide-business/

V. http://blog.bumblebeelabs.com/the-5-guerrilla-user-test/

VI. http://blog.bittorrent.com/2013/04/04/your-book-is-a-startup-tim-ferriss-the-4-hour-chef-and-the-bittorrent-publishing-model/

VII . . http://dictionary.reference.com/browse/empathy

VIII . . http://blog.hubspot.com/blog/tabid/6307/
bid/33800/Photos-on-Facebook-Generate-53-More-
Likes-Than-the-Average-Post-NEW-DATA.aspx

IX . . http://www.mediabistro.com/alltwitter/
infographics-on-twitter_b26840

X . . http://www.copyblogger.com/magnetic-headlines/

Made in the USA
Middletown, DE
05 August 2018